KnockoutJS Blueprints

Learn to design and create amazing web applications using KnockoutJS

Carlo Russo

BIRMINGHAM - MUMBAI

KnockoutJS Blueprints

First published: February 2015

Production reference: 1190215

Published by Packt Publishing Ltd.
Livery Place
35 Livery Street
Birmingham B3 2PB, UK.

ISBN 978-1-78398-084-0

www.packtpub.com

Credits

Author
Carlo Russo

Reviewers
Marko Bojovic

Oscar Finnsson

Marco Franssen

Robert Gaut

Commissioning Editor
Taron Pereira

Acquisition Editor
Owen Roberts

Content Development Editor
Anand Singh

Technical Editor
Ryan Kochery

Copy Editors
Puja Lalwani

Merilyn Pereira

Project Coordinator
Akash Poojary

Proofreaders
Jenny Blake

Paul Hindle

Julie Jackson

Indexer
Tejal Soni

Graphics
Abhinash Sahu

Production Coordinator
Shantanu N. Zagade

Cover Work
Shantanu N. Zagade

About the Author

Carlo Russo works as a consulting software architect and trainer in the field of software development. He started working with computers when he was 15. His dream was to be able to build a video game on his own some day.

He has worked as consultant for many renowned worldwide companies; in his spare time, he develops web applications and learns new programming languages.

In the last 3 years, he worked as a web developer, learning both Angular and DurandalJS; currently, he is focusing on a big Single Page Application built with DurandalJS and Knockout 3.2.

> I would like to thank my wife, Ester Pia, for supporting and
> sustaining me throughout my life and while writing this book.
> She is my life, and I dedicate this book to her.

About the Reviewers

Marko Bojovic graduated in computer science at the University of Milano-Bicocca while building his career. Through the years, he has improved his skills in software engineering and especially in enterprise web applications, primarily (but not only) using Java-based technologies for backend applications. He managed to achieve this by always being in the mainstream in frontend frameworks and best practices.

He worked in different companies where he had the possibility to experiment with specific business needs, such as big data analysis and machine learning techniques. As for his current position, he leads projects as a freelancer while keeping in mind his plan to start his own company in the near future.

> I, for sure, would like to thank my girlfriend, Roberta, for supporting me in this, and I also want to thank Carlo for this opportunity to which I dedicated my full effort.

Oscar Finnsson is a software development consultant at Purepro AB, having previously worked in banking and with payment solutions. He has degrees in engineering physics as well as business administration and economics from Uppsala University.

He is the developer behind pager.js — the most popular Knockout.js plugin at GitHub, which is aimed at large single page web applications.

Marco Franssen is a very passionate developer from the Netherlands. During his career, he has worked on various types of software projects. These projects range from client software and distributed systems to web applications and MS Office add-ins. Some of the techniques and languages Marco is familiar with are C#, ASP.NET MVC, CQRS, DDD, JavaScript, NodeJS, SCRUM, Agile, and so on.

In all of these projects, he worked as a lead developer or architect. Thanks to his ability to think in terms of abstracts, his understanding of processes, and his analytical skills, he was able to achieve success in all of his projects.

He believes that when you master the software design patterns, the choice of programming language actually doesn't matter anymore, since you will be able to learn new programming languages very quickly.

Marco also has a personal weblog at `http://marcofranssen.nl`, where he shares his knowledge with the community.

He has also worked on the book *jQuery Flot Visual Data Analysis*.

Robert Gaut is a father, husband, musician, photographer, martial artist, and software developer. He began his career teaching application and database development at a technical college. After several years of teaching, he spent more than a decade developing web-based content management systems for the automotive industry. He currently works for a large public school district, where he develops business applications and data integration processes using Microsoft technologies.

www.PacktPub.com

Support files, eBooks, discount offers, and more

For support files and downloads related to your book, please visit www.PacktPub.com.

Did you know that Packt offers eBook versions of every book published, with PDF and ePub files available? You can upgrade to the eBook version at www.PacktPub.com and as a print book customer, you are entitled to a discount on the eBook copy. Get in touch with us at service@packtpub.com for more details.

At www.PacktPub.com, you can also read a collection of free technical articles, sign up for a range of free newsletters and receive exclusive discounts and offers on Packt books and eBooks.

https://www2.packtpub.com/books/subscription/packtlib

Do you need instant solutions to your IT questions? PacktLib is Packt's online digital book library. Here, you can search, access, and read Packt's entire library of books.

Why subscribe?

- Fully searchable across every book published by Packt
- Copy and paste, print, and bookmark content
- On demand and accessible via a web browser

Free access for Packt account holders

If you have an account with Packt at www.PacktPub.com, you can use this to access PacktLib today and view 9 entirely free books. Simply use your login credentials for immediate access.

Table of Contents

Preface

In the past five years, almost everyone working on web applications has used jQuery; but when you start working with a more complex app, you understand how difficult it is to work in such a low-level way. This is the reason behind KnockoutJS — to help you to build Rich Web Application by thinking in a high-level way, with models and not worrying about the DOM anymore. In this way, you can think about products to show, user profiles, and working days, not about table rows and columns, and you can scale up in complexity easily.

This book starts with a simple project to show you how to use all the basic features of KnockoutJS, then it will go through four other projects, to teach you how to use this library in different contexts.

The goal of this book is to teach you how to create fully testable web applications from real-world solutions with the powerful data-binding offered by KnockoutJS, how to bind all the components of a web application together — no matter how big it is, how to create new reusable components by yourself, and how to integrate external libraries easily.

What this book covers

Chapter 1, From Idea to Realization, introduces you to the structure of a basic KnockoutJS application. It's a good introduction, and it shows how KnockoutJS implements the data-binding.

Chapter 2, Starting Small and Growing in a Modular Way, shows you how to realize a BookingOnline website. We'll see how to realize template and component, and we will use RequireJS to modularize our code.

Chapter 3, SPA for Timesheet Management, shows how you to realize an SPA with DurandalJS (which uses KnockoutJS as a data-binding library).

Chapter 4, Tracking Expense Using PhoneGap, goes in a different direction by using Cordova to build a hybrid mobile application. We will use KnockoutJS with jQuery Mobile and Jasmine to show you how to test a MVVM application realized with KnockoutJS.

Chapter 5, Wizard for the Public Administration, realizes another SPA, keeping in mind accessibility and SEO.

What you need for this book

Since this book is mostly about client-side code, the main tools required are a text editor and a browser. However, the realization of hybrid mobile application with Cordova needs a working Node.js installation.

You'll have to install Node.JS (`http://nodejs.org`), which comes with npm, the Node package manager.

It can be useful to use http-server (a node application) to serve the web application we realize, because the browsers have many limitations when you access them using the file:// protocol.

Who this book is for

If you are a JavaScript developer and already know the basics of KnockoutJS and you want to get the most out of it, then this book is for you. This book will help you transition from a small site to a large web application that is easily maintainable.

Conventions

In this book, you will find a number of text styles that distinguish between different kinds of information. Here are some examples of these styles and an explanation of their meaning.

Code words in text, database table names, folder names, filenames, file extensions, pathnames, dummy URLs, user input, and Twitter handles are shown as follows: "We can include other contexts through the use of the `include` directive."

A block of code is set as follows:

```
myViewModel.categories = ko.computed(function() {
  var results = myViewModel.allCategories(),
      filterByCategory = myViewModel.selectedCategory();
  if (filterByCategory) {
    results = ko.utils.arrayFilter(results, function(category) {
      return category.name === filterByCategory;
    });
  }
  return results;
});
```

When we wish to draw your attention to a particular part of a code block, the relevant lines or items are set in bold:

```
var myViewModel = {
  allCategories: ko.observableArray([]),
  selectedCategory: ko.observable(),
  selectedName: ko.observable("")
};
```

Any command-line input or output is written as follows:

```
# npm install -g http-server
```

New terms and **important words** are shown in bold. Words that you see on the screen, for example, in menus or dialog boxes, appear in the text like this: "Here we get the starting page, with an **Error loading page**."

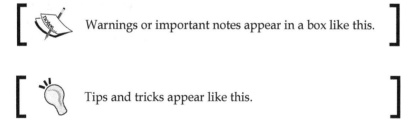

> Warnings or important notes appear in a box like this.

> Tips and tricks appear like this.

Reader feedback

Feedback from our readers is always welcome. Let us know what you think about this book—what you liked or disliked. Reader feedback is important for us as it helps us develop titles that you will really get the most out of.

To send us general feedback, simply e-mail feedback@packtpub.com, and mention the book's title in the subject of your message.

If there is a topic that you have expertise in and you are interested in either writing or contributing to a book, see our author guide at www.packtpub.com/authors

Customer support

Now that you are the proud owner of a Packt book, we have a number of things to help you to get the most from your purchase.

Downloading the example code

You can download the example code files from your account at http://www.packtpub.com for all the Packt Publishing books you have purchased. If you purchased this book elsewhere, you can visit http://www.packtpub.com/support and register to have the files e-mailed directly to you.

Downloading the color images of this book

We also provide you with a PDF file that has color images of the screenshots/diagrams used in this book. The color images will help you better understand the changes in the output. You can download this file from https://www.packtpub.com/sites/default/files/downloads/0840OS_Graphics.pdf.

Errata

Although we have taken every care to ensure the accuracy of our content, mistakes do happen. If you find a mistake in one of our books—maybe a mistake in the text or the code—we would be grateful if you could report this to us. By doing so, you can save other readers from frustration and help us improve subsequent versions of this book. If you find any errata, please report them by visiting http://www.packtpub. com/submit-errata, selecting your book, clicking on the **Errata Submission Form** link, and entering the details of your errata. Once your errata are verified, your submission will be accepted and the errata will be uploaded to our website or added to any list of existing errata under the Errata section of that title.

To view the previously submitted errata, go to https://www.packtpub.com/books/ content/support and enter the name of the book in the search field. The required information will appear under the **Errata** section.

Piracy

Piracy of copyrighted material on the Internet is an ongoing problem across all media. At Packt, we take the protection of our copyright and licenses very seriously. If you come across any illegal copies of our works in any form on the Internet, please provide us with the location address or website name immediately so that we can pursue a remedy.

Please contact us at copyright@packtpub.com with a link to the suspected pirated material.

We appreciate your help in protecting our authors and our ability to bring you valuable content.

Questions

If you have a problem with any aspect of this book, you can contact us at questions@packtpub.com, and we will do our best to address the problem.

1
From Idea to Realization

In this chapter, we are going to assume that your experience with KnockoutJS is very minimal; here, we will introduce how to get it and start using it. We will also learn the philosophy behind this great library and the pattern, **Model-View-ViewModel (MVVM)**.

We will learn all this while building a simple, small e-commerce web application and we will see why everything is easier when you work thinking about *models* instead of **document object model (DOM)** nodes.

By the end of this chapter you'll know:

- What KnockoutJS is
- What are and how to use KnockoutJS observables, computed observables, and data binding
- What benefits the MVVM design pattern gives you
- The magic behind this library
- How to apply MVVM using KnockoutJS

If you already know how to use KnockoutJS, you can take a quick read through this chapter.

What KnockoutJS is and where you can get it

KnockoutJS is a JavaScript library that helps build web applications easily.

It's not a framework, so it's wrong to try to compare it with other web development frameworks like Angular or Ember or Backbone; with KnockoutJS you don't find anything to help you with multiple-page applications, routing, or the interface your server should have.

If you are searching for a framework to build an **Single Page Application** (**SPA**), you could have a look at **DurandalJS**, which extends the capability of KnockoutJS with features (like routing) that you need to build an SPA.

KnockoutJS is, at its heart, a data-binding library for the web.

It means that it helps you to keep synchronized your web pages (written in HTML) with JavaScript objects. In this way, you can think about the models you want to show and how they interact with each other, instead of thinking about the structure of the page and how to get the information from there.

The website of this library is `http://knockoutjs.com/`.

You can download the KnockoutJS library from this link: `http://knockoutjs.com/downloads/index.html`.

In this book, we are going to use the latest version available at the time the book is being written, so here is the direct link to download it: `http://knockoutjs.com/downloads/knockout-3.2.0.js`.

The library we use is the minified version. You can find also a non-minified one, but use it only if you want to learn better how KnockoutJS works internally; as suggested on the download page, don't use it for normal application development, because it exposes additional unsupported private APIs.

 Before we move on, if you haven't done so yet, please try the live tutorial on using KnockoutJS, which you can find here: `http://learn.knockoutjs.com/`. You will learn the basic usage of KnockoutJS, and you'll find this book easier to understand.

The idea of this chapter – Simple Show Case

You have a couple of friends who enjoy making and selling jewelry, and they want your help creating a website so that they can sell online.

We start by asking them what they really need to give us an idea to build a first prototype.

They want to show all products together, and provide a way to filter them based on the category (for example, necklaces, rings, and so on), or by name; sorting by price can be a nice addition (but we will decide later if we will implement this feature or not).

Each product should have also a section with the description, with one or more big images, the price, and a buy button.

They want also a contact page, and a page with the list of the items the customer wants to buy.

If it were possible, they would also like to sell directly from the website, getting the payment in their bank account.

From these requirements we can understand that we have to realize:

- A starting page with the full list of products and one/many filter(s)
- A detailed page for each product
- A contact page
- A cart

The name of this prototype will be `SimpleShowCase`.

The bare bone code of a KnockoutJS application

I'm sure you have seen a lot of web applications with all the JavaScript code in the main HTML page. As a web developer, I suggest you avoid this kind of behavior.

 A good practice when you develop any web application is to divide the visual code (HTML) from the scripting code; one reason is that HTML pages are hard to test, and if you fill them with inner code you will have a hard time fixing bugs caused by JavaScript.

There are different ways to organize your code, and in another chapter, we will look at how can you use the RequireJS library to modularize it; but just now, for this first simple application, we don't need the overhead that library introduces.

Here, we will put all the HTML pages in the root folder, the style sheet files in a folder named css, and all the JavaScript inside a js folder.

Let's start making a folder called SimpleShowCase, with these sub-folders:

* js
* images

Then, in the SimpleShowCase folder, create the following files:

* index.html
* js/index.js

You can save empty files just now, or, if you are using a Unix-like OS you can use the program, touch, in this way:

```
touch SimpleShowCase/index.html
```

You must also put the downloaded library, knockout.js, as SimpleShowCase/js/knockout.js (download it now if you skipped this step before).

On Windows, you should have something like this:

If you have a Unix-like system (Linux, Mac OS X), you should have a structure like this:

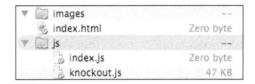

Finally, download from the website the `StartingPackage.zip` for this chapter, and decompress it in the `SimpleShowCase` folder; you'll get all the images and a style sheet file realized by our designer.

Now, we can start with the code for the index page; put this starting markup into `index.html`:

```html
<!DOCTYPE html>
<html>
<head>
  <title>Jewelry Show Case</title>
  <link rel="stylesheet" href="css/styles.css" />
</head>
<body>
  <h1>Welcome to our Jewelry collection.</h1>
  <h2>Can you find anything interesting?</h2>
  <div data-bind="foreach: jewels">
    <div class="jewel">
      <span data-bind="text: name"></span>
      <img data-bind="attr: { src: src }">
```

```
      </div>
    </div>
    <script type="text/javascript" src="js/knockout.js"></script>
    <script type="text/javascript" src="js/index.js"></script>
  </body>
</html>
```

Here, we are asking the browser to:

- Load the stylesheet file
- Create a really simple DOM structure
- Load the KnockoutJS library and `js/index.js`, which contains our application code.

On this page, we put three different kind of data-binding attributes from the standard codebase of KnockoutJS: **foreach**, **text**, and **attr**.

The details about these binding handlers are as follows:

- `foreach`: This is used with an array property and replicates the DOM structure inside the node it is applied to; it creates a node for each item in the array and assigns the context to the specific item; for example, in our application, for each jewel a `div` element is created
- `text`: This binds to the `innerText` data of the node
- `attr`: This is a hash map and binds every item inside it to the property of the node

Our view is ready, but if you try to look at the application with a web browser you'll find that nothing magical is going on. The reason is that we need another major step to get everything working: **applying the bindings**.

So, now we go to our application code in `js/index.js` and we put these lines:

```
var myViewModel = {
  jewels: ko.observableArray([
    { name: "White Bracelet",
      src: "images/bracelet_1_big_1.png" },
    { name: "Tear Earring",
      src: "images/earring_1_big_1.png" },
    { name: "Gold Necklace",
```

```
        src: "images/necklace_1_big_1.png" },
    { name: "Marriage Ring",
        src: "images/ring_2_big_1.png" }
  ])
};
ko.applyBindings(myViewModel);
```

Here, we are making our View Model object (nothing more than a normal JavaScript object, defined with the object literal syntax) with only one property: `jewels`.

The value of the property is `ko.observableArray()`; this is a helper inside the **ko namespace** that KnockoutJS gives us to create observable properties for the array type. You can get much more information about it at this link: `http://knockoutjs.com/documentation/observables.html`.

The value you pass into the call to `ko.observableArray` is the starting value of this object; here, we are creating it with an array with four items.

> The `ko.observableArray` value is an implementation of the Decorator design pattern. In fact, it decorates your array with some logic to detect the changes (while implementing the Observable design pattern).

Anyway, the true magic of KnockoutJS starts with the next row:

```
ko.applyBindings(myViewModel);
```

In the next section, we will see what this function does in depth, but now, to get some code running, we can simply say it binds the view model object with the DOM.

Getting jQuery because it can be useful

In the previous section, we put the data directly inside the View Model; this was just to show how the ViewModel works. In any normal application the source of your data is online and you get it by calling a remote service.

Anyway, as you can see if you look at the documentation of KnockoutJS, the library doesn't provide you any help to take the data. We could use plain JavaScript to do this; but to make it a little easier, we will be using `jQuery` to deal with our AJAX request in the rest of the book.

Browser compatibility

One of the most relevant features of KnockoutJS is its browser compatibility; it even works on ancient browsers, so you can use it if you need to support them.

When you develop a big application to be used online you have to decide which browser you're going to support; the main reason is that each browser you decide to support means:

- Testing on it
- Checking if your code/style sheet/HTML page can be supported, and how

For this reason, many big companies keep an eye on the browser market share data; it helps you to decide if it's time to drop support for a particular browser.

I mentioned this here because we are going to use jQuery. This library is different from KnockoutJS, because you must choose between two branches: 1.x and 2.x.

The main difference here is the compatibility; if you want to support all the browsers KnockoutJS supports you have to download the 1.x branch, otherwise you can choose 2.x.

 For these chapters, we will use the 1.x branch (we will use 1.11.1). You can download the latest jQuery library here: http://code. jquery.com/jquery-1.11.1.min.js.

After you download it, save it as SimpleShowCase/js/jquery.js.

Then update the index page to include it before the row where we included KnockoutJS:

```
</div>
<script type="text/javascript" src="js/jquery.js"></script>

<script type="text/javascript" src="js/knockout.js"></script>
```

Understanding MVVM, MVP, and MVC to get the best

When you start to look at the documentation on KnockoutJS, before getting an explanation on what an observable is and how it works, you get the explanation of the presentation pattern that is used with KnockoutJS. You can live without this explanation, but it can help you to understand why we are using it and how you should organize your project when you use this pattern.

As you can read on the KnockoutJS website, MVVM is a design pattern for building user interfaces. Here, you can find a short description about this pattern and what each term means. Instead of repeating the same information, I suggest you check this URL before moving on: `http://knockoutjs.com/documentation/observables.html#mvvm_and_view_models`.

Let's discuss this design pattern in more detail in the following section. To understand what MVVM is and why someone invented this pattern, we have to discuss its origin: **Model-View-Controller** (**MVC**).

MVC (Model-View-Controller)

MVC is an architectural design pattern that enforces separation of concern; it isolates business data (models) from the user interface (views) using a third component (controllers) which manages the logic and the user input, and coordinates the models and the views.

It was a really well-done pattern, but then we changed context, and we needed a pattern for the web.

There are a few server-side implementations of MVC for the web, and in each of them you can find how the controllers stay on the server, managing the user input, modifying the model, and then sending a new view to the client.

The main drawback of this kind of implementation is that you can find it a bit static and not so responsive.

The first way people solved this problem was by using AJAX heavily to update the client without refreshing the page; in this way, you get all the benefits of server MVCs in the context of the web development.

After that, a new kind of application was built: SPA. In such an application, you use a client router which manages the transition between pages directly on the client-side, keeping all the states and reusing all the information the client already has, avoiding a data trip from the server to the client for each request.

Then, a new problem arose: too much complexity and spaghetti code to keep the client and server synchronized, using jQuery and AJAX.

So a large number of new client-side MVC frameworks were born, mainly done with JavaScript.

The client-side implementation of MVC is realized in this way:

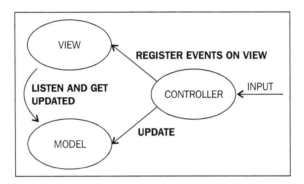

In this implementation, the **Models** and the **Controllers** are JavaScript objects, and the **Views** are HTML.

The Models keep the data, the Views show the information to the user getting the data from the Models, and the Controllers manage the user interaction and the update of the Models.

The main drawbacks of this structure are:

- The Views know about the Models; they listen to the Models to show the most updated data. This means we are tightly coupling Views and Controllers (so a change to one affects the other), and they are closely coupled to the Models (a change to the Model affects both the View and the Controller).

- The Controllers have to register the interaction of the Views by themselves, so they are full of interaction code instead of having all the management logic.

- Another consequence of the previous point; the Views are tightly coupled with the Controllers because the most commonly used way to reference the Views element is by ID with jQuery selectors, and any changes to the DOM structure will impact the relative Controller.

I'm not saying MVC is not a good pattern, but that maybe we can find something better for web development.

MVVM (Model-View-View Model) to the rescue

And then John Grossman from Microsoft built another architectural design pattern (as a specialization of Martin Fowler's Presentation Model design pattern): MVVM.

The main idea behind this pattern is that in the MVC the View knows too much about the Model, and someone should manage all the data transformation.

Think about this: in our database we keep the date of the creation of a product; when we load our model from the server we get this information, as a Date object. In the view, small.html, we want to show this date with a short format, and in the view big.html we want to show it in the long format; where do you put all this information?

With the MVC you can have a single Date object and the View can have a code-behind converter; or you can have all the three Dates pre-formatted inside the Model; or the Controller can set the format inside the View when it decides which View to show and initialize.

As you can see in this example, a problem with MVC is that all the View-related data not directly found inside the Model has no home.

The MVVM pattern works differently, as you can see in this picture:

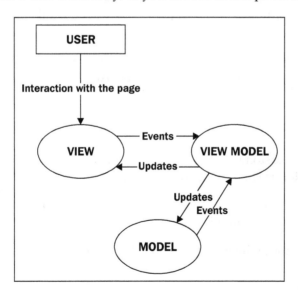

Here, the Model keeps the data from your business logic and works by itself.

The View Model knows the Model, and it can use it and expose it (and other property not Model-related like a date pre-formatted, or the color of the theme if you give the User a way to change it) to whatever View want to use it; and it doesn't need to know anything about the View.

The View ignores the Model, and uses the View Model to get the information to render and to manage the user interaction.

So, briefly, the Views and the Models send events to the View Model, and the View Model updates the Views and the Models directly.

Let's review all the components of this pattern.

Model

The models are the domain objects that we are going to use in the web application.

In our project, we need to represent jewelry products with description, images, and so on; so our models will be **Product** (to describe the name, the description, the images, and all the other data related to our jewelry), **Category** (because all the products will have a category, and each category should have a name and other information), **Cart** (because it will be the container of the product the customer wants to buy).

In a more generic vision, the Models are all the objects you think about when you have to describe your product; in a web application you get them from the server, maybe in a database.

Another kind of model data is the information about the user. Let's think about a website with a registration form; in that case the user data will be part of the model, and probably you'll create a model class, **User**.

View

The interface to the customer is the View; it can be done with HTML and CSS, or it can be the user interface of a client application.

When you use KnockoutJS, your Views will be done with HTML and you'll put data-bind attributes to relate to the View Model.

The page, `index.html`, which we wrote in the previous section, is one of the Views we will make.

View Model

The View Model exposes to the View a subset of the data of the Model (but often it exposes the entire Model object) and all the specific data for the View.

Try to think about `index view` and `product detail view`.

We have the same Model for both the views, but in `index view` we show only a thumbnail of the product, and in `product detail view` we show only the big images.

In MVVM, the View doesn't need a reference to the View Model, nor the View Model should know there is a View, because the data binding library will keep both synchronized.

A really good consequence of this last point is that you can easily test the View Models and Models without having to mock any View.

Data binding

When you use this pattern, you need a library to manage the data binding; it gives a way to loose couple View and View Model and to keep them synchronized.

Data binding is really useful and simplifies your code because of the separation of the concern; the main drawback of this functionality is that it generates a small overhead; let's understand why.

You have a View Model with an observable property, `name`.

 The data binding design pattern is deeply bound to the Observer pattern; KnockoutJS maps the observables using the data-bind attribute, and the observers are the View Model properties.

When you define this property, the data binding system must keep this information: **List of observers**

Now, use the data binding inside your View to use the name (`data-bind="text:name"`); the system, to manage this binding, must:

- Create a context object (an object keeping references to the parent context, to the root context, and to the data)
- Evaluate the expression inside the context (in this case, a property, but it can be a full expression)
- Add itself to the list of observers for each referred observable found inside the expression

So, just for this binding, we are adding:

- **Memory occupation**: A list with an item and an object with at least three properties (parent, root, and data)
- **CPU**: The creation of the context and the evaluation of the binding

As you can see, when you build really big application you must start thinking about which object should be observable, to optimize the system.

Let's recap the pros and the cons of using MVVM:

- Pros:
    ◦ Separated concerns
    ◦ Better testability of business and application code
    ◦ Low coupling between components, which gives more freedom to the UI designer to redesign a webpage without the fear of breaking everything

- Cons:
    ◦ Memory occupation and CPU overhead caused from data binding logic.

I hope now you understand this pattern better and how to use it in the best way.

We will see better what you should put inside each component during development.

Getting data from the server

After a long explanation without any code, before you get really bored, let's update our code to use a real data source for the product.

In a real web application, we probably should have a database and a server-side REST API, which can be used to retrieve the data.

In the future, we may give your friend a full web interface to update the product data, and maybe we will add a true database as the backend, but at the moment, we will simply use a JSON file with all the products.

Pay attention when you want to use the jQuery function, getJSON; many browsers (such as Chrome) won't permit you to load JSON from the local file system because they need a web server.

You can use any web server you like, but if you plan to read the fifth chapter, I suggest you to try to use NodeJS and the package, http-server.

Installing NodeJS is really simple (you can use the installer); then you can get the http-server package with the following command (in the command line):

npm install -g http-server

Then, go to the SimpleShowCase folder and execute:

http-server

And now, you have a working web server (you can see the port in the console output) serving your files (at http://localhost:port). You can now use getJSON without any problem.

You will find a file named products.json inside the folder, SimpleShowCase, with all the products we can show (with descriptions and images); check it to see the structure of the JSON.

Now, we can update our View Model to use these products; we will remove all the fake data we put inside the View Model, and fill it with the data from the external JSON:

```
var myViewModel = {
  categories: ko.observableArray([])
};

$.getJSON("products.json", function(data) {
  myViewModel.categories(data.categories);
});

ko.applyBindings(myViewModel);
```

We renamed the property from jewels to categories because now we are showing categories.

Here, we have loaded the data from the JSON into the View Model; now we have to update the View to show the new data.

Before modifying the code, open the page, `index.html`, with a web browser; you should see only the category, `Necklaces`.

This not a problem with the data, but with the data binding; you have no idea of the problem, because KnockoutJS simply stopped working, without any visual information. So, open the developer tool, firebug, or any console you have in your browser.

 Chrome, Firefox, and the latest version of Internet Explorer give you the console using the *F12* key, if you're using Windows. To get the console on the Mac OS X, use *Alt+Cmd+I* for Chrome and *Alt+Cmd+K* for Firefox.

You should have something like this (this screenshot was taken on the Mac OS X with Safari):

Welcome to our Jewelry collection.

Can you find anything interesting?

Necklaces

```
⊕ ReferenceError: Unable to process binding "attr: function () {return { src:src} }"
  Message: Can't find variable: src
>
```

KnockoutJS is saying it tried to apply the binding, and it died trying to apply it to the data bind, `attr: function()  { return { src: src} }`, because it cannot find the variable, `src`, inside the current context of the View Model.

We will discuss binding context in detail in the next section, when we will reveal how KnockoutJS works internally.

 Remember to check the browser console when you see strange behaviors but think your code is right; KnockoutJS logs all errors with the `console.error` function, so you'll find them there.

We will modify the code we rendered for each item, because now we want to show the category, then the list of products; so, we will replace the following markup:

```
<div data-bind="foreach: jewels">
  <div class="jewel">
    <span data-bind="text: name"></span>
    <img data-bind="attr: { src: src }">
  </div>
</div>
```

With this markup:

```
<div data-bind="foreach: categories">
  <div class="category">
    <h3>Category: <span data-bind="text: name"></span></h3>
    <div data-bind="foreach: products">
      <div class="jewel">
        <div data-bind="text: title"></div>
        <img data-bind="attr: { src: 'images/' + thumb }">
      </div>
    </div>
  </div>
</div>
```

Here, we have two `foreach`, two `text`, and an `attr` data binding. They are more in number than before, but, at the end, we are using the same kind of data binding, so there's nothing really special here.

 Downloading the example code

You can download the example code files from your account at http://www.packtpub.com for all the Packt Publishing books you have purchased. If you purchased this book elsewhere, you can visit http://www.packtpub.com/support and register to have the files e-mailed directly to you.

The current results should be as in this image, right?

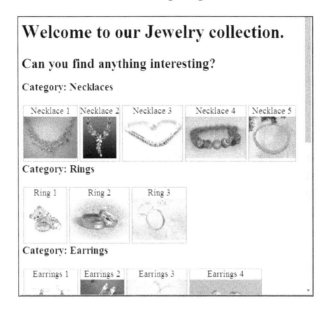

Your results can be different if you didn't download the `SimpleShowCase/products.json` file and the content of the `SimpleShowCase/images` folder from the website.

Now, we have a page with all the products listed under the categories.

We could improve this page by adding filters, or maybe we could learn how KnockoutJS works internally. What do you prefer? Really? Perfect, let's start.

The magic of KnockoutJS unveiled

We saw that all the magic of KnockoutJS starts with the call to:

```
ko.applyBindings(myViewModel);
```

This function gets two parameters: a View Model and a DOM element. You can skip the second parameter and it will default to the `document.body`.

First of all, it takes the View Model, and makes a `ko.bindingContext` from the View Model.

BindingContext tracks all the following information:

- `$parent`: This is the View Model of the parent context; for example, every binding inside a foreach binding will have the foreach view model as $parent

- `$parents`: This refers to an array with all the parents context; empty for the root View Model. You can use an indexer to traverse the hierarchy (for deep-nesting); for instance, $parents[1] will get you the 2nd ancestor and so on

- `$root`: This is the View Model of the highest parent; itself for the root view model.

- `$rawData`: This is the original View Model, before unwrapping (to understand "unwrapping" better, imagine that you have a property, x = `ko.observable(12)`, and you execute `x()`; you are unwrapping the observable to get the value `12`)

- `$data`: This refers to the unwrapped View Model.

Then, it starts to apply the bindings to the node:

- It stores the `bindingContext` inside the node data (but only if the current context is different from the context inside the parent node)

- It checks if the current node contains the data-bind attribute, and applies the binding to each of them

- For each binding, it executes the **init** function inside a call to **ko. dependencyDetection.ignore**, and then the **update** function inside a call to **ko.dependentObservable**; in this way, the update function of each binding handler works as a computed observable (more about computed observables a little later)

- It executes these steps recursively for each descendant

Binding to the same node more than once is not permitted; when you call `ko.applyBindings` it checks if the node is already bound and it will throw an exception.

When you think you need to apply the binding again (maybe you changed the DOM structure without KnockoutJS) to the same node, the best idea is to rethink why you should do it; often you will see you can use the **with** binding handler to solve this problem in a KnockoutJS way.

Or, if you are absolutely sure this is the best solution, you can use `ko.cleanNode` to reset the element to its previously unbound state.

The change of the `bindingContext` is done inside a few binding handlers (`with`, `foreach`, and so on) because they create a child `bindingContext`; you can do the same inside your custom binding handler's `init` function (for more information visit this URL: `http://knockoutjs.com/documentation/custom-bindings-controlling-descendant-bindings.html`).

> Before looking at a practical example, let's understand what a computed observable is.
>
> `ko.computed` is the third kind of Observable KnockoutJS supports; it's defined by a function, and each time it runs it registers itself as subscriber of any Observable found during the evaluation.
>
> This is the same method KnockoutJS uses for the binding handler you find in the View.
>
> In a few words, a computed observable is an observer of another observer; the easiest example is the full name computed observable, defined as the concatenation of the observable, name, and the observable, last name:
>
> ```
> var firstName = ko.observable("Bob"),
>     lastName = ko.observable("Smith");
> var fullName = ko.computed(function() {
>     return firstName() + " " + lastName();
> });
> ```
>
> The property `fullName` here gets evaluated each time one of its internal observables changes.

Let's understand step by step what happens when you execute `ko.bindingHandler(viewModel)` in the current document.

We start with the following DOM structure:

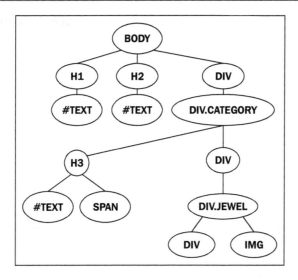

As the first step, it takes the document.body node to work on, as you can see in the following picture:

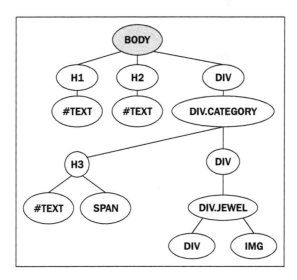

It creates and adds to the data of the node, body, a new `BindingContext` like this:

```
ko.bindingContext: {
    $root: obj,
    $rawData: obj,
    $parents: [],
    $data: obj
}
```

Here `obj` is the parameter, `viewModel`.

Then it walks inside the descendants searching for the `data-bind` attribute; the next node to work on is the following one:

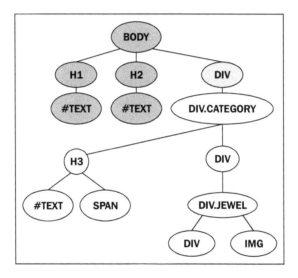

Here it finds a `foreach` binding, so it executes the binding handler; the `init` function returns **controlsDescendantBindings**, so it stops descending.

The function `init` of `foreach` saves the descendants and clears the DOM structure, so now we have this structure:

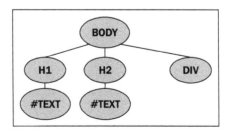

After this step it ends, because all the descendants of `document.body` are bound to our view model.

When the code updates `viewModel.jewels` with the content of the category list, the flow continues.

Filters and product details

Now that you know how KnockoutJS works, we can continue working on the website.

The next step in the requirements is to add a way to filter the products by the category or by the name.

At the moment, we are showing all the products; to show only filtered products we have to:

- Save the data from the server in a new variable called `allCategories`
- Add a new observable to keep the selected category, and a new array to keep the list of the names of categories; we will add the "All" value using the **optionsCaption** binding handler (a binding handler dependent on the selected binding handler).
- Add a new observable to keep the selected name
- Create a computed observable to return the array of categories based on the selected category and the list of all categories

Before we start to write the code, I want to point out that there are two different ways to manage the last point in the preceding list. You can:

- Use an observable array and, with an external computed observable, update that array
- Use a computed observable which will do the job of filtering and then return an array

If you look at the documentation of KnockoutJS you will find:

Assuming your array is an observable array, whenever you later add, remove, or re-order array entries, the binding will efficiently update the UI to match - inserting or removing more copies of the markup, or re-ordering existing DOM elements, without affecting any other DOM elements. This is far faster than regenerating the entire foreach output after each array change.

The first observation after reading this is that the `foreach` binding handler uses the notification from the observable array to discover what changed.

But if you check the code of the binding, you will be astonished, because you will find an algorithm to check the difference between the current array and the previous one, ignoring all the notifications from the observable array.

For this reason, the previously pointed solutions work in the same way.

Let's update the View Model (`js/index.js`) with all the changes we need for the filters:

```
var myViewModel = {
  allCategories: ko.observableArray([]),
  selectedCategory: ko.observable(),
  selectedName: ko.observable("")
};
```

We will rename the old observable array, `categories`, as `allCategories`, and also add two observables to keep the new filter variable: `selectedCategory` and `selectedName`.

> `ko.observable` is another kind of Observable KnockoutJS gives us; when you declare an observable it keeps a list of observers, subscribed to any change of that value.
>
> Other than using (getting and setting) the value in the observable, you can subscribe (using the method `subscribe`) to execute a callback each time the value changes. The result is like the computed observable, but you are responsible for deciding when to dispose the subscription.
>
> To find more information you can look at the excellent documentation of this functionality.

Then, we will create our computed observable to return the filtered array. We cannot insert this code directly in the object creation because KnockoutJS will execute the code to pre-assign the value, so we need to define the other properties before this one:

```
myViewModel.categories = ko.computed(function() {
  var results = myViewModel.allCategories(),
      filterByCategory = myViewModel.selectedCategory();
  if (filterByCategory) {
    results = ko.utils.arrayFilter(results, function(category) {
      return category.name === filterByCategory;
```

```
    });
  }
  return results;
});
```

 A good, easy way to improve the code, solving also this last point, is the use of the JavaScript Module Pattern. We are not using it here because this project is really simple, but if you don't know it, now is a good time to study it; it will help you to understand the next chapter better.

This code takes the list of categories (`allCategories`) and the selected filter (`selectedCategory`).

If a filter was selected, we assume that the first item in the list having a name equal to the selected category which we return.

Here, you can see we are using the function, `ko.utils.arrayFilter`. This is just one of the many helper functions you can find in the namespace, `ko.utils`. It is unlikely that they are not documented at all, so you can:

- Search information on the web
- Look at the non-minified source file (but pay attention, a few functions you find there are not accessible when you use the minified version)

With this function, we get a filtered array with any item having a name the same as our selected category.

Add the following property after the **myViewModel.categories** definition:

```
myViewModel.categoryName = ko.computed(function() {
    var results = ko.utils.arrayMap(myViewModel.allCategories(),
function(category) {
        return category.name;
    });
    return results;
});
```

We will now add a list of the names of all the categories using the mapping function (`ko.utils.arrayMap` is good for "flattening" an array or extracting a subset of data into an array).

Then, we will put back the code to take the products from the server, but this time we will save them in the `allCategories` property.

```
$.getJSON("products.json", function(data) {
  myViewModel.allCategories(data.categories);
});

ko.applyBindings(myViewModel);
```

Now, we will use all these new properties in our View (`index.html`). We will add these rows after the first tag H2, to keep the filter on the top of the page:

```
<div class="filter">
  <h2>Filter by</h2>
  <div class="category">
    Category:
    <select data-bind="options: categoryName,
                       optionsCaption: 'All',
                       value: selectedCategory"></select>
  </div>
  <div class="name">
    Name:
    <input type="text" data-bind="textInput: selectedName" />
  </div>
</div>
```

We are binding three handlers to the select:

- `options: categories`: A new option tag will be created for each item inside the array

- `optionsCaption: 'All'`: Another option with the selected text and `undefined` value will be added as first child of the select tag

- `value: selectedCategory`: The value of the selected option will be bound to that property

We also bound the input with `textInput: selectedName`; this binding handler is a new introduction, added in version 3.2. In the previous version, you used a combination of `value` and `updateValue:'input'` but in the current version, as you can read in the documentation, this is the best way to get a two-way binding into the input field.

When you use the `options` binding handler, you can use two additional useful binding handlers: `optionsText` and `optionsValue`; they are useful when the items inside the array used with the `options` binding handler are JavaScript objects and you want to choose what to use as value (optionsValue) and as text (optionsText) of the `option` tag.

To complete the filtering code, we will change the following row:

```
<div class="jewel">
```

By adding this data binding:

```
data-bind="visible: title.indexOf($root.selectedName()) !== -1"
```

Now, it will hide all the items not containing the text of the selected item inside the name.

The reason we are using `$root` is because here we are inside the `foreach` context, so we have to move to the parent context to find the property, `selectedName`.

Everything is done, so we can continue with the product details, right?

Wrong!

Look again at the last data bind: `visible: title.indexOf($root.selectedName()) !== -1`.

What's the problem with this code? I'm sure you have seen it many times in the past; so, why am I telling you it is wrong?

Do you remember when I suggested to you to avoid putting JavaScript code inside the HTML? It's the same reason.

KnockoutJS will take the code you put inside the binding and will evaluate it, so that code will work; but now it will become hard to test.

A good practice with data binding is to keep the logic inside the View Model (the main reason we have it) and to keep the View as dumb as you can.

We don't want to modify all the products to keep the information, and our models are simply objects, so we cannot modify the prototype. The easiest way to solve the problem is with a new function inside the View Model, referring the current object; we use it inside a data-bind context, so it will automatically become a computed one.

Let's change the data-bind we added earlier with this code:

```
data-bind="visible: $root.shouldShow($data)"
```

Then, we add this function in the object, `myViewModel`:

```
shouldShow: function(item) {
  return item.title.indexOf(myViewModel.selectedName()) !== -1;
}
```

Now, everything should work again, and our View is dumb again and your browser should show something like this:

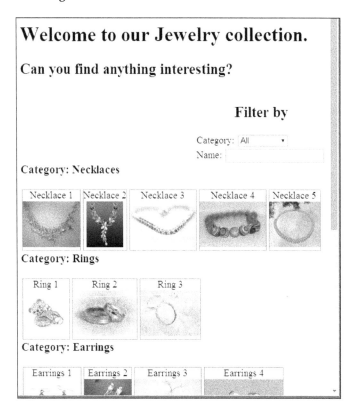

If everything is working, you can change the selected category and the category sections should change.

We used the `indexOf` method to check for the text; if you want to make it case un-sensitive you can replace the following code:

```
return item.title.indexOf(myViewModel.selectedName()) !== -1;
```

With this code:

```
return new RegExp(myViewModel.selectedName(),"gi").test(item.title);
```

Product details

Now, we can add the page for product details. To keep this chapter simple, we will add a box with all the details, and we will show it when the customer **hovers** or **clicks** on the image of a product.

In this box, we will show all the details we decided earlier: the description, one or more big images, the price, and a button to add it to the cart.

First of all, we have to add a new property to keep the selected products. Add the following row to the View Model (`js/index.js`), after the `allProducts` definition:

```
selectedProduct: ko.observable(),
```

Then, add the code of the box to the View (`index.html`); put these lines before the first `script` tag:

```html
<div class="selectedProduct" data-bind="with: selectedProduct">
  Prodotto selezionato:
  <div class="jewel">
    <div data-bind="text: title"></div>
    <!-- ko foreach: images -->
      <img data-bind="attr: { src: 'images/' + $data }">
    <!-- /ko -->
    <div data-bind="text: description"></div>
    <div data-bind="text: price"></div>
    <button>Add to cart</button>
  </div>
</div>
```

Here, we are using the `with` binding handler. This binding handler checks for the parameter, and creates a new child context with the parameter, only if the parameter is not `null`. In this way, we can be sure it will show the selected product only if we select one, and we avoid binding errors if the object does not exist.

In the block, we show the title, all the images, the description, and the price of the product.

With this code we can render the selected product, but we didn't put any way to select it. To do that we will add a new function in the View Model to select the item, another two to show/remove the item under the cursor, a `click` binding, a `mouseout` event binding, and a `mouseover` event binding to the preview tag to call these functions.

Let's add all these functions to the `myViewModel` object:

```
selectProduct: function(product) {
  myViewModel.selectedProduct.current = product;
},
showProduct: function(product) {
  myViewModel.selectedProduct.current =
    myViewModel.selectedProduct();
  myViewModel.selectedProduct(product);
},
hideProduct: function() {
  myViewModel.selectedProduct(
    myViewModel.selectedProduct.current);
}
```

Here, we are adding a property (named `current`) to the observable property, `selectedProduct`, to track which item the customer clicked on. In this way, each time the customer clicks on a preview, we will record it, and we will show it in the detail box; when the customer moves the cursor over a preview she/he will see the new detail, but it will go back to the selected one when the mouse exits from the preview.

Now, add the three binding handlers to the preview. Replace the following row:

```
<div class="jewel" data-bind="visible: $root.shouldShow($data)">
```

With these rows:

```
<div class="jewel"
    data-bind="visible: $root.shouldShow($data),
               click: $root.selectProduct,
               event: {
                   mouseover: $root.showProduct,
                   mouseout: $root.hideProduct
               }">
```

The `click` binding handler registers a click event handler and when the event is fired you will get the View Model and the event as parameters. This is really useful when we are working in a child context, because we get the current item.

We should add here the click handler to the button, `Add to Cart`, but we will do this in the next section.

Now, when you move the mouse over a preview, or you click it, your browser should show something like this:

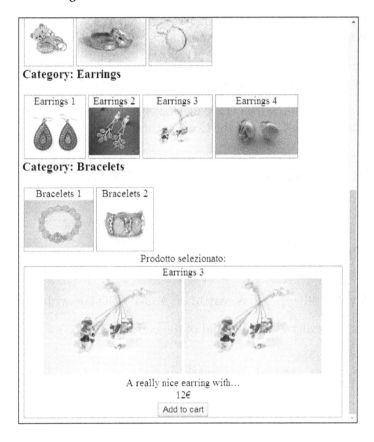

Managing a Cart

When you realize a web application, you can follow two different flows:

- Classic web application
- Single Page Application

If you realize an SPA, you'll probably need something like a library to manage the routing client-side, a way to load an external page with a View Model, and so on.

The best library you can find at the moment to create an SPA with KnockoutJS is DurandalJS. We will see this in another chapter.

If you go to the classic web application, you'll have many different pages, and you will have to apply the binding of KnockoutJS in each page needing it.

In this project, we will follow the classic web application flow, so we will add two new pages to manage the Cart and the Contact form.

Using the Cart on the home page

The modifications we make in the index page include:

- Showing the links to the other pages
- Creating a basket
- Adding a handler to the `Add to cart` button

Adding a link to the other pages is easy to do, so we will start with this.

Add the following rows as the first child of the body (in `index.html`):

```
<div class="topbar">
  <a href="index.html">Home page</a>
  <a href="cart.html">Cart</a>
  <a href="contact_us.html">Contact us</a>
</div>
```

Then, to have a cleaner interface, move the whole following block before the H1 tag:

```
<div class="filter">…</div>
```

Now, we have a navigation bar at the top with the link to the three pages of our application.

To keep this application simple, we will save the basket in the local storage. We are building a really simple application, but this is not a good reason to use a bad pattern, so we will not mix the model of the basket and the storage.

For this reason, we will create two new files:

- `js/basket.js`
- `js/basket-localStorage.js`

We do this because the best practice with Model is that it shouldn't have knowledge of its storage.

We can start with the model of the basket (`js/basket.js`), because at this time it is really simple:

```
function Basket() {
  this.products = ko.observableArray([]);
}

Basket.prototype.addToCart = function(product) {
  this.products.push(product);
};

Basket.prototype.removeFromCart = function(product) {
  this.products.remove(product);
};
```

Here, we are just enclosing an observable array to hide the implementation from outside.

Now, we will create the local storage file (`js/basket-localStorage.js`):

```
var basketLocalStorage = (function() {
  return {
    fetch: function(basket) {
      var json = localStorage.getItem("SimpleShowCase"),
          savedData = JSON.parse(json || "[]");

      ko.utils.arrayForEach(savedData, function(product) {
        basket.addToCart(product);
      });
    },
```

```
    save: function(basket) {
      var data = ko.toJSON(basket.products);
      localStorage.setItem("SimpleShowCase", data);
    }
  };
}());
```

This object now exposes two functions:

- `fetch`: This takes from the local storage the array of products and adds it to the product list
- `save`: This puts into the local storage the product list using the JSON format

A few notes about this last source code:

- We are using `localStorage`; it's an easy way to save data locally, but it works only in modern browsers (so it's good for a simple project, but think twice about using it when you want to support IE6/IE7)
- We are calling `push` on an observable array inside a loop; a better solution should put all the data in one call, because each call to `push` notifies all the observers, resulting in poor performance.

Now, in our main page (`index.html`) we can add a reference to these two new scripts; add these two rows just before the tag with the import of `js/index.js`:

```
<script type="text/javascript" src="js/basket-localStorage.js"></
script>
<script type="text/javascript" src="js/basket.js"></script>
```

As the last step on this page, we have to bind the click on the button, **Add to cart**, to the function. Add the following data bind to the button **Add to cart**:

```
data-bind="click: $root.addToCart"
```

We have to make two modifications to the View Model, `js/index.js`. Add these two rows into the `myViewModel` object:

```
basket: new Basket(),
addToCart: function(product) {
  myViewModel.basket.addToCart(product);
  basketLocalStorage.save(myViewModel.basket);
}
```

In this way, we keep a basket ready and when the user adds an item to the cart we add it to the basket and then save changes in the storage.

We should also load the data from the basket, so add this row at the end of the file:

```
basketLocalStorage.fetch(myViewModel.basket);
```

Here, we ask the storage to load all the data into the basket.

With this last modification our main View is completed, managing all the requirements we had for it.

The Cart page

The cart page will be simpler than the index page. We will show all the elements we have inside the basket, and a button will give the user the option to remove elements from the cart.

Let's start with the Cart View (`cart.html`):

```html
<!DOCTYPE html>
<html>
<head>
  <title>Jewelry Show Case - Cart</title>
  <link rel="stylesheet" href="css/styles.css" />
</head>
<body>
<div class="topbar">
  <a href="index.html">Home page</a>
  <a href="cart.html">Cart</a>
  <a href="contact_us.html">Contact us</a>
</div>
```

This is the standard boilerplate code for the View.

Let's continue with the container for the products:

```html
<h1>Here you can find all the items in the cart.</h1>
<div data-bind="foreach: products">
  <div class="jewel"
    <div data-bind="text: title"></div>
    <img data-bind="attr: { src: "images/" + thumb }">
    <div data-bind="text: description"></div>
    <div data-bind="text: price"></div>
    <button data-bind="click: $root.removeFromCart">
      Remove from the cart</button>
  </div>
</div>
```

Here, we are showing a list of products with their details, and a button to remove the jewelry from the cart.

```
<script type="text/javascript" src="js/jquery.js"></script>
<script type="text/javascript" src="js/knockout.js"></script>
<script type="text/javascript" src="js/basket-localStorage.js"></
script>
<script type="text/javascript" src="js/basket.js"></script>
<script type="text/javascript" src="js/cart.js"></script>
</body>
</html>
```

Then, we will add all the scripts we need (it's really similar to the index page, isn't it?).

Now, let's see the View Model, `js/cart.js`. Here, you can find a few similarities to the other one, but not enough to justify a refactoring of the common code into a parent class:

```
var myViewModel = {
  basket: new Basket(),
  removeFromCart: function(product) {
    myViewModel.basket.removeFromCart(product);
    basketLocalStorage.save(myViewModel.basket);

    if (myViewModel.products().length === 0) {
      window.location.href = 'index.html';
    }
  }
};
myViewModel.products = myViewModel.basket.products;

basketLocalStorage.fetch(myViewModel.basket);

ko.applyBindings(myViewModel);
```

Our View Model references a `Basket` and exposes a `removeFromCart` function.

In this function, we are asking the basket to remove the product, and then saving the modification in the local storage. As the last step, when we empty the cart, we are redirecting the user to the home page.

We are exposing the `products` property of `basket` inside `myViewModel` because we want a dumb View; so, we should not ask the View to know the internal structure of the `basket` Model.

With this, we finally get the product list from the basket storage, with the call to `basketLocalStorage.fetch`.

Now we have a page to add the products to the basket, a page to look at and remove them from the basket. We are only missing a page to send a request to our friends to buy them.

Contact form

Our friends asked us if we could add a way to pay from the website. We can do it for sure, but it involves code in the backend.

For this first project, we are not going to write any code for the backend, so we will not implement this functionality; we will try to keep the flow simple, so we will open the default mail program with pre-configured text.

Paying from the client-side code

If you are thinking, *why do I need a backend code to manage all of this? I have seen on the PayPal website that I can send a payment request using only JavaScript*, let's wait a moment and read this hint:

Never use a Javascript-only solution to manage money.

Have you heard about **XSS**, **CSRF**, and the other threats you can face with website programming?

You can find many good resources about these threats, and I suggest you research them (any good web developer should know about security).

I'll just explain the simpler reason here. JavaScript is a client-side language; it runs within the browser, so any one can hack it easily.

Let's try to imagine this scenario:

A customer puts in his cart three products that are worth £60. Then, he (he's smart, isn't he?) opens the developer console and updates the `localStorage`, setting all the prices to negative value. Next, he navigates to the contact page, and we ask him to use PayPal to pay -£60.

What happens here? It depends on PayPal, or on the payment system you are trying to implement.

In the best case, it stops the transaction (but what if the customer puts £0?). In the worst case, it could grab the money from your account to give it to the customer.

If the system blocks a negative transaction, it can change all the prices to £0 (or £0.01 if it wants to be sure that everything works). The system will accept the transaction, and your friends will get a notification that they have to send a few products to someone without being paid.

So, try to remember that client-side validation is helpful to improve performance and give the user a better experience. But at the end of the day, any data you have to save on a database has to be checked on the server side.

The contact form

We are going to realize a small contact form to send to our friends a mail with the list of products the customer wants to buy.

We cannot send email using only JavaScript, so for this first chapter, we will build the mail body inside our page, and then use the `mailTo:` URL to ask the system to open the preferred mail application with the data we collected.

The customers can fill their email address and the body of the mail, and we will add to the mail the list of the products he wants to buy.

This page will be similar to the cart page, because we will show a list of all selected products. But here, we will not give the user a way to remove the item; we will give him a way to send the email with the items.

This time we will start with the HTML of the Cart View, and then modify it; copy `cart.html` into `contact_us.html`.

Best practices with programming tell us that copying and pasting code is never a good thing; maybe it's an easy way to solve a problem, but then you can make the maintenance hell.

For this reason, when you see you have to put the same code in more than one place, with only small modifications, try to change the structure, use the inheritance or the composition, and avoid copy and paste!

The only time you cannot do this easily is with HTML, because if you load the markup from an external template with jQuery, you face problems with binding and so on.

In the next chapter, we will use the template and the component binding handler, and we will find how to solve the copy-paste problem in HTML.

Then:

- Update the title to `Jewelry Show Case - Contact`

- Remove the H1: `<h1>Here you can find all the items in the cart.</h1>`

- Add the form to get the email address and a message; wrap the entire block `<div data-bind="foreach: products">` in this way:

```
<form data-bind="submit: buy">
  <div class="field">
    My mail address:
    <input type="text" data-bind="textInput: email"/>
  </div>
  <div class="field">
    Additional details:
    <textarea data-bind="value: message"></textarea>
  </div>
  <h1>List of items I would like to buy</h1>
  <div data-bind="foreach: products"></div>
  <div class="clear-float"></div>
  <input type="submit" value="Send the buying message"
         data-bind="enable: canBuy"/>
</form>
```

- We don't want to give the user a way to remove a product here, so remove from the product box the button, `<button data-bind="click: $root.removeFromCart">Remove from the cart</button>`

- Update the script tag `<script type="text/javascript" src="js/cart.js"></script>` with the new script name `<script type="text/javascript" src="js/`**`contact_us.js`**`"></script>`

Let's better analyze the important markup (where we put binding) here:

```
<form data-bind="submit: buy">
```

In this way, we are putting all the data inside a form, and we will execute the buy function when the user submits the form (either by clicking on the submit button or using the enter key).

```
<input type="text" data-bind="textInput: email" />
```

We are using again the `textInput` binding handler because we want to react immediately to the field changes.

```
<textarea data-bind="value: message"></textarea>
```

We are using the `value` binding handler here for the `message` because we are not putting any additional logic based on the value of that field.

```
<input type="submit" value="Send the buying message"
                data-bind="enable: canBuy"/>
```

We are adding the `enable` binding handler to enable/disable the submit button, to be sure that the user has to fill the required email field before trying to send the email.

In this case, the only difference between the submit binding handler and the click binding handler attached to this button is that you can press enter when you are in the email field and the form will be submitted.

Obviously, is important to understand when it is better to use one and when the other, depending on the specific context you are working on.

Now, we can work on the Cart View Model (`js/cart.js`).

This View Model will begin similarly to the Cart View Model because we need to fetch the product list and show the products we have in the basket.

Then, we will add the specific code: two observables, a computed observable, and a function:

```
var myViewModel = {
  basket: new Basket(),
  email: ko.observable(""),
  message: ko.observable(""),
  buy: function() { /* CODE TO SEND THE EMAIL */ }
};
myViewModel.products = myViewModel.basket.products;
myViewModel.canBuy = ko.computed(function() {
  return myViewModel.email() &&
         myViewModel.products().length;
});
basketLocalStorage.fetch(myViewModel.basket);
ko.applyBindings(myViewModel);
```

The canBuy computed observable checks that the email is not empty and that the cart contains at least one item.

Let's check the code of the buy function:

```
buy: function() {
  var productList =
    ko.utils.arrayMap(myViewModel.products(), function(p) {
      return p.title;
    });
  var additionalMessage = myViewModel.message() && (
      "This is an additional message I want to send you: \n\t" +
      myViewModel.message()
  );
  var body = "Hi, I'm " + myViewModel.email() +
             " and I want to buy these products from you.\n" +
             productList + "\n" +
             additionalMessage;
  var mail = "mailto:postmaster@example.com?" +
             "subject=" + encodeURIComponent("I want to buy these
items") +
             "&body=" + encodeURIComponent(body);
  window.location.href = mail;
}
```

Here, we are taking the name of each product we have in the cart, the message, and the email, and putting it into an encoded string. We must encode it because otherwise we cannot use it inside a URL.

Then, we will use this string with the protocol, `mailto`, and update the current URL with this new one.

When we do this, the browser will try to open the default mail program to send this email.

Now, the **Contact Us** page is complete and you can use it to create the email with the messages and the products you want to buy.

If you have done everything like I have suggested, this is what you should get when you put three products in the cart and you are ready to send the mail:

And this is what we get after we click on the button (having Gmail registered as the default mail system, with Chrome in Windows):

Here, it opens Gmail with the information we entered in the form, as we expected.

Summary

In this chapter, we have seen what the MVVM pattern is about and how KnockoutJS implements this pattern to provide you with data-binding capabilities. We realized the application was really simple, but we saw many features of KnockoutJS regardless.

We used three different types of observables (`observable`, `observableArray`, and `computed`). We also saw many different binding handlers and utility functions.

Best of all, we learned how to create a full-featured application using View Model and data binding. There are a few binding handlers we haven't seen, like `template` or `component`, but we will see them in the next chapter, and there we will create new custom binding handlers too.

2
Starting Small and Growing in a Modular Way

Another small project will be realized; it will show all the features of KnockoutJS we skipped in the previous chapter, including templates and components, to give you a 360 degree view of this great library.

The topics that will be covered in this chapter include:

- Exploring **templates**, **components,** and all the other binding handlers
- Making new and useful binding handlers
- Modularizing what we realize, looking at **AMD** and the usage of **RequireJS**

At the end of this chapter you should be able to create a modular application well integrated with external libraries.

Analyzing the project – booking online

The project we are going to realize in this chapter is an online booking site.

Let's imagine you get hired by a company doing online booking, because their site is good, but they know you can make it superlative.

You will work with many other great developers so you will have all the backend functionalities you need; you can also ignore all the problems with the styles, because other people will take care of them; the only thing they need from you is a good, bug-free, web interface.

This domain is new for us, so as the first step, we will go around looking at the website of many competitors, to get an idea about what users can expect from such sites.

This is the list of the competitors we are studying for ideas:

- Booking.com (`http://www.booking.com/`)
- AirBnB (`https://www.airbnb.it/`)
- Expedia (`http://www.expedia.it/`)
- Trivago (`http://www.trivago.it/`)
- Hotels.com (`http://www.hotels.com/`)
- Venere.com (`http://www.venere.com/`)

You can see that all of them share the same structure, only with many visual differences between them.

The first component we get is the `Search Form`.

After that, depending on the searched item, you get a big list of cards, with the details of the hotel, the price, and the availability for the searched dates; we will show them as a list of `Card`.

This is a wireframe of what we should build here:

Building the structure of our application

This project will be an SPA-like web application; it will not be a true SPA because we will not use a client router for a different state; we will just hide and show the components depending on the states of the fields.

Let's start making a folder called BookingOnline, with these sub-folders and empty files:

- app
- app/binding-handlers
- app/components
- app/index.js
- index.html

In the previous chapter, we used a folder named js, but this time we are going to name it app because we will put inside both, the JavaScript and the templates.

In this chapter, we will create custom binding handlers and components; for this reason, we are creating folders for them.

Finally, download from the Packt Publishing website the StartingPackage.zip for this chapter, and decompress it inside the BookingOnline folder; you'll get all the images and a style sheet file realized from our designer.

We will now create the following boilerplate, as we have done in the previous chapter, inside the BookingOnline folder; let's create the main HTML file (BookingOnline/index.html) with this starting markup:

```
<!DOCTYPE html>
<html>
<head>
  <title>Booking Online - smaller and cheaper</title>
  <link rel="stylesheet" href="css/styles.css" />
</head>
<body>
  <h1>Why should you choose us?</h1>
  <h2>Just because we are a really small startup, so we can do really
competitive prices!!!</h2>

<script src="app/jquery.js"></script>
<script src="app/knockout.js"></script>
<script src="app/index.js"></script>
</body>
</html>
```

This starting code will be the starting page for our shining web application.

Before going to work on the first component, the `Search Form`, it's better to look at what a **component** is, and how describe it using KnockoutJS.

Modularizing with the component binding handler

In this section, we are going to discuss two different concepts:

- AMD and RequireJS
- KnockoutJS binding handler called `component`

The reason we are going to look at them together is because the best way to use the second one is with the help of the first one.

AMD and RequireJS

Asynchronous Module Definition (**AMD**) is a way to modularize JavaScript; you can get a good overview of what AMD is and why it is a good idea to use it at this URL: `http://requirejs.org/docs/whyamd.html`.

Before the use of AMD, all HTML pages were full of script tags to import all the scripts used. You have seen this behavior in the previous chapter, when we put five script tags into each HTML page.

One of the goals of AMD is to improve the separation of JavaScript and HTML; we get this because we put only one script tag in the HTML file, representing the main entrance to our client-side application. Inside this entrance file we put all the logic to load the other components, with their dependencies.

Another goal of AMD is to avoid the pollution of the global namespace. Many JavaScript applications and libraries put all the variables inside the global namespace (window, if you are working within the browser).

When you use AMD, you create self-contained modules with a list of required dependencies.

 You can mix modules and global variables, but you should avoid it, because it is evil. Moreover, there is no way to be sure your global variable will not be overwritten, or modified, from external code.

AMD defines two functions: `define` and `require`.

Use `define` to declare a new module; look how a simple module can be declared with dependencies over two other modules (for example, jQuery and KnockoutJS):

```
define(["jquery", "knockout"], function($, ko) {
    ...
});
```

In this case, the first parameter of `define` is an array of dependencies; this means that the implementation of AMD will load the modules with name `jquery` and `knockout`, and then it will execute the function, `function($, ko)`, passing the modules loaded as parameters (dependency injection).

 Pay attention to the order of the parameters and the items inside the array; AMD associates the dependencies by position, and it will not warn you if you put more parameters than dependencies or the opposite, nor will it check for the name of the module.

The second function we have is `require`; we can use it to load modules dynamically (like a module dependent on a previously loaded module) or to get reference to an already loaded library; this is how we can use it in the first way:

```
define(["jquery", "knockout"], function($, ko) {
    ...
    require(["jqueryui"], function(ui) {
        //do something with dep3
    });
    ...
});
```

In this way you can postpone the loading of a dependency.

 This is an easy way to lazy-load a resource-demanding module or a configuration-based one; for example, you can use it when you want to load the localization module for a library (such as the `jQuery DatePicker Widget`) depending on the current locale.

Let's now look at the second way to use it.

Imagine you already loaded the module dep3 inside the previous module; then, in another module you can enter the following code:

```
define(["jquery", "knockout"], function($, ko) {
    ...
    ui = require("jqueryui");
    ...
});
```

Pay attention that in this way we are making a synchronous request, because AMD will use the already loaded module, so you don't need to put any callback.

> The synchronous version of the require function uses a string as the first parameter, while the asynchronous version uses an array.

In this book we are going to use RequireJS, because it is well documented. You can find a lot of documentation on the optimizer r.js, and how you can mix it with many external libraries. Moreover, you can find a quick explanation about its usage with KnockoutJS on the KnockoutJS website.

> AMD is just a specification, so if you want to use it inside your project you need to use a real implementation; you can find many by searching on the Internet (for example curl.js, RequireJS).

The easiest way to understand how it works is by using it with real code; so let's update our starting code to use this new library.

Updating starting code to use RequireJS

The starting point to understand how to use RequireJS with KnockoutJS is at this URL: http://knockoutjs.com/documentation/amd-loading.html.

As the first step, we will go to the website to download this library; you can get the latest one at this URL: http://requirejs.org/docs/release/2.1.15/minified/require.js.

Save it inside our `app` folder as `BookingOnline/app/require.js`.

A really useful plugin we will need later for RequireJS is `text`; get it from this URL (`http://raw.github.com/requirejs/text/latest/text.js`) and save it as `BookingOnline/app/text.js`.

This plugin is great for loading external HTML templates, which we will use in the next paragraph.

As the latest step to integrate the library with our project, we must update the main HTML file `BookingOnline/index.html` to use it.

Substitute these rows:

```
<script src="app/jquery.js"></script>
<script src="app/knockout.js"></script>
<script src="app/index.js"></script>
```

With this single row:

```
<script src="app/require.js" data-main="app/index.js"></script>
```

What does this mean? Here, we are loading the library with a normal script tag, but we are using a custom parameter; when the library will be loaded, it will search for the `data-main` attribute and will use that attribute to get the application entry point.

This means that the browser will load RequireJS inside the normal browser workflow, and RequireJS will start the loading of the `app/index.js` file asynchronously.

Now, we can put inside our entry point the code required to load KnockoutJS; put this code inside `app/index.js` as follows:

```
define(["jquery", "knockout"], function ($, ko) {
    var viewModel = {};

    $(function () {
        ko.applyBindings(viewModel);
    });
});
```

Here we are:

1. Asking RequireJS to load `jquery` and `knockout`.

2. Executing the following function passing as parameters, the return value from the two modules being loaded.

3. Applying the binding of KnockoutJS after the complete loading of the DOM.

 The RequireJS convention about module loading uses the name to find the file; when you ask for the `jquery` module it will search for a file called `jquery.js` inside the current folder (or inside the `baseUrl`, if you configured it).

RequireJS gives us a simplified format to require many parameters and to avoid parameter mismatch using the CommonJS require format; for example, another way (use this or the other one) to write the previous code is:

```
define(function(require) {
    var $ = require("jquery"),
        ko = require("knockout"),
        viewModel = {};

    $(function() {
        ko.applyBindings(viewModel);
    });
});
```

In this way, we skip the dependencies definition, and RequireJS will add all the texts `require('xxx')` found in the function to the dependency list.

The second way is better because it is cleaner and you cannot mismatch dependency names with named function arguments.

For example, imagine you have a long list of dependencies; you add one or remove one, and you miss removing the relative function parameter. You now have a hard-to-find bug.

And, in case you think that r.js optimizer behaves differently, I just want to assure you that it's not so; you can use both ways without any concern regarding optimization.

Just to remind you, you cannot use this form if you want to load scripts dynamically or by depending on variable value; for example, this code will not work:

```
var mod = require(someCondition ? "a" : "b");
if (someCondition) {
    var a = require('a');
} else {
    var a = require('a1');
}
```

You can learn more about this compatibility problem at this URL: http://www.requirejs.org/docs/whyamd.html#commonjscompat.

You can see more about this sugar syntax at this URL: http://www.requirejs.org/docs/whyamd.html#sugar.

Now that you know the basic way to use RequireJS, let's look at the next concept.

Component binding handler

The component binding handler is one of the new features introduced in Version 2.3 of KnockoutJS.

Inside the documentation of KnockoutJS, we find the following explanation:

Components are a powerful, clean way of organizing your UI code into self-contained, reusable chunks. They can represent individual controls/widgets, or entire sections of your application.

A component is a combination of HTML and JavaScript. The main idea behind their inclusion was to create full-featured, reusable components, with one or more points of extensibility.

> A component is a combination of HTML and JavaScript.
> There are cases where you can use just one of them, but normally you'll use both.

You can get a first simple example about this here: `http://knockoutjs.com/documentation/component-binding.html`.

The best way to create self-contained components is with the use of an AMD module loader, such as RequireJS; put the View Model and the template of the component inside two different files, and then you can use it from your code really easily.

Creating the bare bones of a custom module

Writing a custom module of KnockoutJS with RequireJS is a 4-step process:

1. Creating the JavaScript file for the View Model.
2. Creating the HTML file for the template of the View.
3. Registering the component with KnockoutJS.
4. Using it inside another View.

> We are going to build bases for the Search Form component, just to move forward with our project; anyway, this is the starting code we should use for each component that we write from scratch.

Let's cover all of these steps.

Creating the JavaScript file for the View Model

We start with the View Model of this component. Create a new empty file with the name `BookingOnline/app/components/search.js` and put this code inside it:

```
define(function(require) {
  var ko = require("knockout"),
```

```
    template = require("text!./search.html");

  function Search() {}

  return {
    viewModel: Search,
    template: template
  };
});
```

Here, we are creating a constructor called `Search` that we will fill later.

We are also using the `text` plugin for RequireJS to get the template `search.html` from the current folder, into the argument `template`.

Then, we will return an object with the constructor and the template, using the format needed from KnockoutJS to use as a component.

Creating the HTML file for the template of the View

In the View Model we required a View called `search.html` in the same folder. At the moment, we don't have any code to put inside the template of the View, because there is no boilerplate code needed; but we must create the file, otherwise RequireJS will break with an error.

Create a new file called `BookingOnline/app/components/search.html` with the following content:

```
<div>Hello Search</div>
```

Registering the component with KnockoutJS

When you use components, there are two different ways to give KnockoutJS a way to find your component:

- Using the function `ko.components.register`
- Implementing a custom component loader

The first way is the easiest one: using the default component loader of KnockoutJS.

To use it with our component you should just put the following row inside the `BookingOnline/app/index.js` file, just before the row `$(function () {:`

```
ko.components.register("search", {require: "components/search"});
```

Here, we are registering a module called `search`, and we are telling KnockoutJS that it will have to find all the information it needs using an AMD `require` for the path `components/search` (so it will load the file `BookingOnline/app/components/search.js`).

You can find more information and a really good example about a custom component loader at: `http://knockoutjs.com/documentation/component-loaders.html#example-1-a-component-loader-that-sets-up-naming-conventions`.

Using it inside another View

Now, we can simply use the new component inside our View; put the following code inside our Index View (`BookingOnline/index.html`), before the script tag:

```
<div data-bind="component: 'search'"></div>
```

Here, we are using the `component` binding handler to use the component; another commonly used way is with custom elements.

We can replace the previous row with the following one:

```
<search></search>
```

KnockoutJS will use our search component, but with a WebComponent-like code.

> If you want to support IE6-8 you should register the WebComponents you are going to use before the HTML parser can find them. Normally, this job is done inside the `ko.components.register` function call, but, if you are putting your script tag at the end of body as we have done until now, your WebComponent will be discarded.
>
> Follow the guidelines mentioned here when you want to support IE6-8: `http://knockoutjs.com/documentation/component-custom-elements.html#note-custom-elements-and-internet-explorer-6-to-8`

Now, you can open your web application and you should see the text, `Hello Search`.

We put that markup only to check whether everything was working here, so you can remove it now.

Writing the Search Form component

Now that we know how to create a component, and we put the base of our Search Form component, we can try to look for the requirements for this component.

A designer will review the View later, so we need to keep it simple to avoid the need for multiple changes later.

From our analysis, we find that our competitors use these components:

- Autocomplete field for the city
- Calendar fields for check-in and check-out
- Selection field for the number of rooms, number of adults and number of children, and age of children

This is a wireframe of what we should build (we got inspired by Trivago):

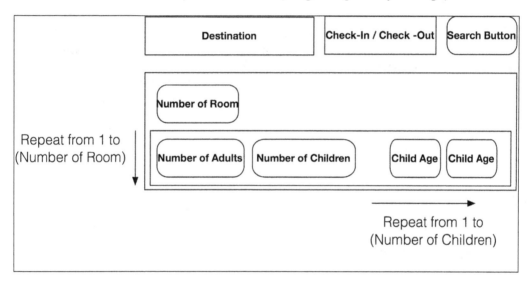

We could do everything by ourselves, but the easiest way to realize this component is with the help of a few external plugins; we are already using jQuery, so the most obvious idea is to use jQuery UI to get the Autocomplete Widget, the Date Picker Widget, and maybe even the Button Widget.

Adding the AMD version of jQuery UI to the project

Let's start downloading the current version of jQuery UI (1.11.1); the best thing about this version is that it is one of the first versions that supports AMD natively.

> After reading the documentation of jQuery UI for the AMD (URL: `http://learn.jquery.com/jquery-ui/environments/amd/`) you may think that you can get the AMD version using the download link from the home page. However, if you try that you will get just a package with only the concatenated source; for this reason, if you want the AMD source file, you will have to go directly to GitHub or use Bower.

Download the package from `https://github.com/jquery/jquery-ui/archive/1.11.1.zip` and extract it.

> Every time you use an external library, remember to check the compatibility support. In jQuery UI 1.11.1, as you can see in the release notes, they removed the support for IE7; so we must decide whether we want to support IE6 and 7 by adding specific workarounds inside our code, or we want to remove the support for those two browsers.

For our project, we need to put the following folders into these destinations:

- `jquery-ui-1.11.1/ui -> BookingOnline/app/ui`
- `jquery-ui-1.11.1/theme/base -> BookingOnline/css/ui`

We are going to apply the widget by JavaScript, so the only remaining step to integrate jQuery UI is the insertion of the style sheet inside our application.

We do this by adding the following rows to the top of our custom style sheet file (`BookingOnline/css/styles.css`):

```
@import url("ui/core.css");
@import url("ui/menu.css");

@import url("ui/autocomplete.css");
@import url("ui/button.css");
@import url("ui/datepicker.css");

@import url("ui/theme.css");
```

Now, we are ready to add the widgets to our web application.

You can find more information about jQuery UI and AMD at: `http://learn.jquery.com/jquery-ui/environments/amd/`

Making the skeleton from the wireframe

We want to give to the user a really nice user experience, but as the first step we can use the wireframe we put before to create a skeleton of the Search Form.

Replace the entire content with a form inside the file `BookingOnline/components/search.html`:

```
<form data-bind="submit: execute"></form>
```

Then, we add the blocks inside the form, step by step, to realize the entire wireframe:

```
<div>
  <input type="text" placeholder="Enter a destination" />

  <label> Check In: <input type="text" /> </label>
  <label> Check Out: <input type="text" /> </label>
  <input type="submit" data-bind="enable: isValid" />
</div>
```

Here, we built the first row of the wireframe; we will bind data to each field later.

We bound the `execute` function to the submit event (`submit: execute`), and a validity check to the button (`enable: isValid`); for now we will create them empty.

Update the View Model (`search.js`) by adding this code inside the constructor:

```
this.isValid = ko.computed(function() {
  return true;
}, this);
```

And add this function to the `Search` prototype:

```
Search.prototype.execute = function() { };
```

This is because the validity of the form will depend on the status of the destination field and of the check-in date and check-out date; we will update later, in the next paragraphs.

Now, we can continue with the wireframe, with the second block. Here, we should have a field to select the number of rooms, and a block for each room.

Add the following markup inside the form, after the previous one, for the second row to the View (`search.html`):

```
<div>
  <fieldset>
    <legend>Rooms</legend>
    <label>
      Number of Room
      <select data-bind="options: rangeOfRooms,
                         value: numberOfRooms">
      </select>
    </label>
    <!-- ko foreach: rooms -->
      <fieldset>
        <legend>
          Room <span data-bind="text: roomNumber"></span>
        </legend>
      </fieldset>
    <!-- /ko -->
  </fieldset>
</div>
```

In this markup we are asking the user to choose between the values found inside the array `rangeOfRooms`, to save the selection inside a property called `numberOfRooms`, and to show a frame for each room of the array `rooms` with the room number, `roomNumber`.

> When developing and we want to check the status of the system, the easiest way to do it is with a simple item inside a View bound to the JSON of a View Model.
>
> Put the following code inside the View (`search.html`):
>
> ```
> <pre data-bind="text: ko.toJSON($data, null,
> 2)"></pre>
> ```
>
> With this code, you can check the status of the system with any change directly in the printed JSON.
>
> You can find more information about `ko.toJSON` at `http://knockoutjs.com/documentation/json-data.html`

Update the View Model (`search.js`) by adding this code inside the constructor:

```
this.rooms = ko.observableArray([]);

this.numberOfRooms = ko.computed({
  read: function() {
    return this.rooms().length;
  },
  write: function(value) {
    var previousValue = this.rooms().length;

    if (value > previousValue) {
      for (var i = previousValue; i < value; i++) {
        this.rooms.push(new Room(i + 1));
      }
    } else {
      this.rooms().splice(value);
      this.rooms.valueHasMutated();
    }
  },
  owner: this
});
```

Here, we are creating the array of rooms, and a property to update the array properly. If the new value is bigger than the previous value it adds to the array the missing item using the constructor `Room`; otherwise, it removes the exceeding items from the array.

To get this code working we have to create a module, `Room`, and we have to require it here; update the `require` block in this way:

```
var ko = require("knockout"),
    template = require("text!./search.html"),
    Room = require("room");
```

Also, add this property to the `Search` prototype:

```
Search.prototype.rangeOfRooms = ko.utils.range(1, 10);
```

Here, we are asking KnockoutJS for an array with the values from the given range.

 ko.utils.range is a useful method to get an array of integers. Internally, it simply makes an array from the first parameter to the second one; but if you use it inside a computed field and the parameters are observable, it re-evaluates and updates the returning array.

Now, we have to create the View Model of the `Room` module. Create a new file `BookingOnline/app/room.js` with the following starting code:

```
define(function(require) {
  var ko = require("knockout");

  function Room(roomNumber) {
    this.roomNumber = roomNumber;
  }

  return Room;
});
```

Now, our web application should appear like so:

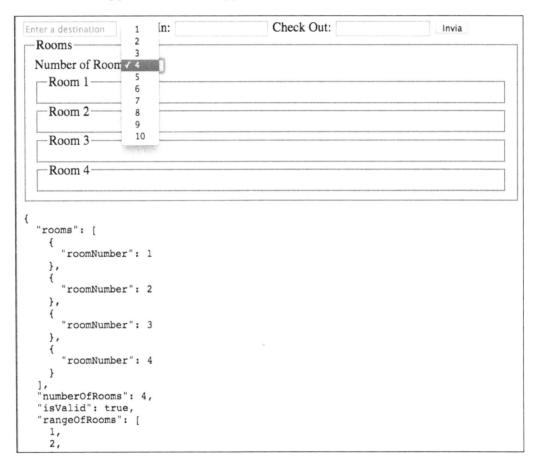

As you can see, we now have a `fieldset` for each room, so we can work on the template of the single room.

Here, you can also see in action the previous tip about the `pre` field with the JSON data.

> With KnockoutJS 3.2 it is harder to decide when it's better to use a normal template or a component.
>
> The rule of thumb is to identify the degree of encapsulation you want to manage:
>
> - Use the component when you want a self-enclosed black box, or the template if you want to manage the View Model directly.

What we want to show for each room is:

- Room number
- Number of adults
- Number of children
- Age of each child

We can update the Room View Model (`room.js`) by adding this code into the constructor:

```
this.numberOfAdults = ko.observable(2);
this.ageOfChildren = ko.observableArray([]);

this.numberOfChildren = ko.computed({
  read: function() {
    return this.ageOfChildren().length;
  },
  write: function(value) {
    var previousValue = this.ageOfChildren().length;

    if (value > previousValue) {
      for (var i = previousValue; i < value; i++) {
```

```
            this.ageOfChildren.push(ko.observable(0));
        }
    } else {
        this.ageOfChildren().splice(value);       this.ageOfChildren.
valueHasMutated();
        }
    },
    owner: this
});

this.hasChildren = ko.computed(function() {
    return this.numberOfChildren() > 0;
}, this);
```

We used the same logic we have used before for the mapping between the count of the room and the count property, to have an array of age of children.

We also created a hasChildren property to know whether we have to show the box for the age of children inside the View.

We have to add — as we have done before for the Search View Model — a few properties to the Room prototype:

```
Room.prototype.rangeOfAdults = ko.utils.range(1, 10);

Room.prototype.rangeOfChildren = ko.utils.range(0, 10);

Room.prototype.rangeOfAge = ko.utils.range(0, 17);
```

These are the ranges we show inside the relative select.

Now, as the last step, we have to put the template for the room in search.html; add this code inside the fieldset tag, after the legend tag (as you can see here, with the external markup):

```
        <fieldset>
          <legend>
            Room <span data-bind="text: roomNumber"></span>
          </legend>
          <label> Number of adults
            <select data-bind="options: rangeOfAdults,
```

```
                                    value: numberOfAdults"></select>
      </label>
      <label> Number of children
        <select data-bind="options: rangeOfChildren,
                            value: numberOfChildren"></select>
      </label>
      <fieldset data-bind="visible: hasChildren">
        <legend>Age of children</legend>
        <!-- ko foreach: ageOfChildren -->
          <select data-bind="options: $parent.rangeOfAge,
                             value: $rawData"></select>
        <!-- /ko -->
      </fieldset>
    </fieldset>
    <!-- /ko -->
```

Here, we are using the properties we have just defined.

We are using rangeOfAge from $parent because inside foreach we changed context, and the property, rangeOfAge, is inside the Room context.

Why did I use $rawData to bind the value of the age of the children instead of $data?

The reason is that ageOfChildren is an array of observables without any container. If you use $data, KnockoutJS will unwrap the observable, making it one-way bound; but if you use $rawData, you will skip the unwrapping and get the two-way data binding we need here. In fact, if we use the one-way data binding our model won't get updated at all.

If you really don't like that the fieldset for children goes to the next row when it appears, you can change the fieldset by adding a class, like this:

```
<fieldset class="inline" data-bind="visible: hasChildren">
```

Now, your application should appear as follows:

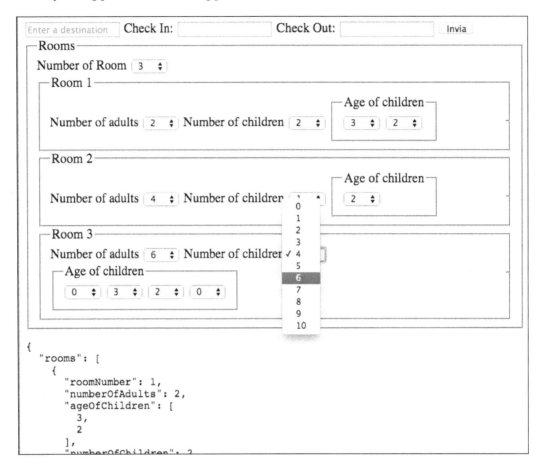

Now that we have a really nice starting form, we can update the three main fields to use the jQuery UI Widgets.

Realizing an Autocomplete field for the destination

As soon as we start to write the code for this field we face the first problem: how can we get the data from the backend?

Our team told us that we don't have to care about the backend, so we speak to the backend team to know how to get the data.

After ten minutes we get three files with the code for all the calls to the backend; all we have to do is to download these files (we already got them with the Starting Package, to avoid another download), and use the function `getDestinationByTerm` inside the module, `services/rest`.

Before writing the code for the field let's think about which behavior we want for it:

- When you put three or more letters, it will ask the server for the list of items
- Each recurrence of the text inside the field into each item should be bold
- When you select an item, a new button should appear to clear the selection
- If the current selected item and the text inside the field are different when the focus exits from the field, it should be cleared
- The data should be taken using the function, `getDestinationByTerm`, inside the module, `services/rest`

The documentation of KnockoutJS also explains how to create custom binding handlers in the context of RequireJS.

The what and why about binding handlers

All the bindings we use inside our View are based on the KnockoutJS default binding handler.

The idea behind a binding handler is that you should put all the code to manage the DOM inside a component different from the View Model. Other than this, the binding handler should be realized with reusability in mind, so it's always better not to hard-code application logic inside.

The KnockoutJS documentation about standard binding is already really good, and you can find many explanations about its inner working in the *Appendix, Binding Handler*.

When you make a custom binding handler it is important to remember that: it is your job to clean after; you should register event handling inside the `init` function; and you should use the `update` function to update the DOM depending on the change of the observables.

This is the standard boilerplate code when you use RequireJS:

```
define(function(require) {
  var ko = require("knockout"),
      $ = require("jquery");

  ko.bindingHandlers.customBindingHandler = {
    init: function(element, valueAccessor,
                   allBindingsAccessor, data, context) {
      /* Code for the initialization… */

      ko.utils.domNodeDisposal.addDisposeCallback(element,
        function () { /* Cleaning code … */ });
    },
    update: function (element, valueAccessor) {
      /* Code for the update of the DOM… */
    }
  };
});
```

And inside the View Model module you should require this module, as follows:

```
require('binding-handlers/customBindingHandler');
```

`ko.utils.domNodeDisposal` is a list of callbacks to be executed when the element is removed from the DOM; it's necessary because it's where you have to put the code to destroy the widgets, or remove the event handlers.

Binding handler for the jQuery Autocomplete widget

So, now we can write our binding handler.

We will define a binding handler named autocomplete, which takes the observable to put the found value.

We will also define two custom bindings, without any logic, to work as placeholders for the parameters we will send to the main binding handler.

Our binding handler should:

1. Get the value for the `autoCompleteOptions` and `autoCompleteEvents` optional data bindings.

2. Apply the Autocomplete Widget to the item using the option of the previous step.

3. Register all the event listeners.

4. Register the disposal of the Widget.

We also should ensure that if the observable gets cleared, the input field gets cleared too.

So, this is the code of the binding handler to put inside BookingOnline/app/ binding-handlers/autocomplete.js (I put comments between the code to make it easier to understand):

```
define(function(require) {
    var ko = require("knockout"),
        $ = require("jquery"),
        autocomplete = require("ui/autocomplete");

    ko.bindingHandlers.autoComplete = {
        init: function(element, valueAccessor, allBindingsAccessor, data,
context) {
```

Here, we are giving the name autoComplete to the new binding handler, and we are also loading the Autocomplete Widget of jQuery UI:

```
var value = ko.utils.unwrapObservable(valueAccessor()),
    allBindings = ko.utils.unwrapObservable(allBindingsAccessor()),
    options = allBindings.autoCompleteOptions || {},
    events = allBindings.autoCompleteEvents || {},
    $element = $(element);
```

Then, we take the data from the binding for the main parameter, and for the optional binding handler; we also put the current element into a jQuery container:

```
autocomplete(options, $element);

if (options._renderItem) {
    var widget = $element.autocomplete("instance");
    widget._renderItem = options._renderItem;
}

for (var event in events) {
    ko.utils.registerEventHandler(element, event, events[event]);
}
```

Now we can apply the Autocomplete Widget to the field.

 If you are questioning why we used `ko.utils.registerEventHandler` here, the answer is: to show you this function. If you look at the source, you can see that under the wood it uses `$.bind` if jQuery is registered; so in our case we could simply use `$.bind` or `$.on` without any problem.

But I wanted to show you this function because sometimes you use KnockoutJS without jQuery, and you can use it to support event handling of every supported browser.

The source code of the function `_renderItem` is (looking at the file `ui/autocomplete.js`):

```
_renderItem: function( ul, item ) {
    return $( "<li>" ).text( item.label ).appendTo( ul );
},
```

As you can see, for security reasons, it uses the function text to avoid any possible code injection.

 Web development and security is a really big argument and we will see it better in another chapter; at the moment, it is important that you know that you should do data validation each time you get data from an external source and put it in the page.

In this case, the source of data is already secured (because we manage it), so we override the normal behavior, to also show the HTML tag for the bold part of the text.

In the last three rows we put a cycle to check for events and we register them.

 The standard way to register for events is with the event binding handler. The only reason you should use a custom helper is to give to the developer of the View a way to register events more than once.

Then, we add to the `init` function the disposal code:

```
// handle disposal
ko.utils.domNodeDisposal.addDisposeCallback(element, function() {
    $element.autocomplete("destroy");
});
```

Here, we use the `destroy` function of the widget.

> It's really important to clean up after the use of any jQuery UI Widget or you'll create a really bad memory leak; it's not a big problem with simple applications, but it will be a really big problem if you realize an SPA.

Now, we can add the `update` function:

```
    },
    update: function(element, valueAccessor) {
      var value = valueAccessor(),
          $element = $(element),
          data = value();

      if (!data)
        $element.val("");
    }
  };
});
```

Here, we read the value of the observable, and clean the field if the observable is empty.

> The `update` function is executed as a computed observable, so we must be sure that we subscribe to the observables required inside. So, pay attention if you put conditional code before the subscription, because your `update` function could be not called anymore.

Now that the binding is ready, we should require it inside our form; update the View `search.html` by modifying the following row:

```
<input type="text" placeholder="Enter a destination" />
```

Into this:

```
<input type="text" placeholder="Enter a destination"
       data-bind="autoComplete: destination,
                  autoCompleteEvents: destination.events,
                  autoCompleteOptions: destination.options" />
```

If you try the application you will not see any error; the reason is that KnockoutJS ignores any data binding not registered inside the `ko.bindingHandlers` object, and we didn't require the binding handler `autocomplete` module.

So, the last step to get everything working is the update of the View Model of the component; add these rows at the top of the search.js, with the other require(...) rows:

```
Room = require("room"),
rest = require("services/rest");
require("binding-handlers/autocomplete");
```

We need a reference to our new binding handler, and a reference to the rest object to use it as source of data.

Now, we must declare the properties we used inside our data binding; add all these properties to the constructor as shown in the following code:

```
this.destination = ko.observable();
this.destination.options = {
  minLength: 3,
  source: rest.getDestinationByTerm,
  select: function(event, data) {
    this.destination(data.item);
  }.bind(this),
  _renderItem: function(ul, item) {
    return $("<li>").append(item.label).appendTo(ul);
  }
};
this.destination.events = {
  blur: function(event) {
    if (this.destination() && (event.currentTarget.value !==
                              this.destination().value)) {
      this.destination(undefined);
    }
  }.bind(this)
};
```

Here, we are defining the container (destination) for the data selected inside the field, an object (destination.options) with any property we want to pass to the Autocomplete Widget (you can check all the documentation at: http://api.jqueryui.com/autocomplete/), and an object (destination.events) with any event we want to apply to the field.

Here, we are clearing the field if the text inside the field and the content of the saved data (inside `destination`) are different.

> Have you noticed `.bind(this)` in the previous code? You can check by yourself that the value of `this` inside these functions is the input field.
>
> As you can see, in our code we put references to the `destination` property of `this`, so we have to update the context to be the object itself; the easiest way to do this is with a simple call to the `bind` function.
>
> Remember that the `bind` function doesn't work with IE6 and IE7, so if you want to use it, try the jQuery function `$.proxy`.

This is a screenshot of the current application:

When we show this screenshot to our boss we get an *OK, it's nice, but can we put a small clearing icon after the user selects an item?*

Obviously we cannot say *no*; and… *why?* With KnockoutJS it's so easy to add.

We start to do it in the easiest way, like a prototype: code inside the View and inside the ViewModel.

As the first step, we update the View, search.html, adding the following rows after the input field for the destination:

```
<span data-bind="visible: destination.isNotEmpty,
                 click: destination.clear">
  <i class="ui-icon ui-icon-circle-close"> </i>
</span>
```

It's simply an icon (from jQuery UI, inside the ui/theme.css) with a binding to know when to show and what to do when clicked.

Then we update the View Model, search.js, adding this code just after the definition of destination.events:

```
this.destination.isNotEmpty = ko.computed(function() {
  return this.destination() !== undefined;
}, this);

this.destination.clear = function() {
  this.destination(undefined);
};
```

Now we get a really nice icon inside the field, after we select an item, with the functionality of clearing the selection.

We can also update the validation code to enable the button for the search; change the following block:

```
this.isValid = ko.computed(function() {
  return true;
}, this);
```

Into this one:

```
this.isValid = ko.computed(function() {
  return this.destination();
}, this);
```

And be sure you have this computed function defined after the definition of the property, destination, or you'll get an error.

With this code, we finish all the code for the destination field.

Improving two date fields by applying Date Picker widget

If you followed the whole previous paragraph you will have seen how to create a binding handler for a jQuery Widget, so we can just apply what we learnt in the previous paragraphs.

Create the file, `BookingOnline/app/binding-handler/datepicker.js`, with this code:

```
define(function(require) {
  var ko = require("knockout"),
      $ = require("jquery");
  require("ui/datepicker");
```

The first difference with the previous binding is with the module, `datepicker`; this one is the only module without a returned value. You must apply it starting from the jQuery selector:

```
ko.bindingHandlers.datepicker = {
  init: function(element, valueAccessor) {
    var value = valueAccessor(),
        $element = $(element);

    $element.datepicker({
      onSelect: function(dateText, inst) {
        value($element.datepicker("getDate"));
      },
      numberOfMonths: 2
    });
```

We apply the `datepicker` to the element, and we register the behavior of the selection. Assign the selected date to the observable used as a parameter for the binding:

```
// handle disposal
ko.utils.domNodeDisposal.addDisposeCallback(element, function() {
  $(element).datepicker("destroy");
});
```

Every jQuery Widget has the same disposal code, only with a different function name (here it is `datepicker`; the previous name was `autocomplete`).

 You could write object-oriented code here, generalizing the name with a string; you can see this kind of logic used in the project *Knockout-jQueryUI* at: `http://gvas.github.io/knockout-jqueryui/`

Then we close the init and continue with the update function:

```
    },
    update: function(element, valueAccessor) {
      var value = valueAccessor(),
          $element = $(element),
          data = value();

      if (!data)
        $element.datepicker("setDate", undefined);
    }
  };
});
```

In the update we clear the field if the observable was cleaned.

The next step is in the View, `search.html`, where we update the two fields for the date. They become:

```
<input type="text" readonly data-bind="datepicker: checkIn" />
```

And:

```
<input type="text" readonly data-bind="datepicker: checkOut" />
```

Finally, we update the View Model, `search.js`; we require the module of the binding handler, after the starting block of `require(...)` in the following way:

```
require("binding-handlers/autocomplete");

require("binding-handlers/datepicker");
```

In the constructor, we add the two observables to track the selected dates:

```
this.checkIn = ko.observable();
this.checkOut = ko.observable();
```

And, as the last step, we update the validation method. It becomes:

```
this.isValid = ko.computed(function() {
  var d = this.destination(),
      cIn = this.checkIn(),
      cOut = this.checkOut();

  return d && cIn && cOut;
}, this);
```

There is a big difference between the following two expressions:

```
var v1 = this.destination(), v2 = this.checkIn();
var res = v1 & v2;
```

And this:

```
var res = this.destination() && this.checkIn();
```

The main difference is that in the second expression, if the destination is false, we'll never check the checkIn observable.

Normally, this is not a big problem, but if any function has important side effects (otherwise you should use a pure-computed observable), remember that you should use the first expression type, not the second one.

Transforming already done code into a reusable one

When the boss asks again for the closing icon, we know we can follow two different ways:

- Copy and paste the code all around, for each field
- Make a new binding handler to manage this functionality

This book is a blueprint, so we must choose the best solution to show the best practice. So we take the piece of HTML we used and the related binding, and we put it in a binding handler.

Why a binding handler instead of a component? It depends.

In this case, a binding handler is better because we want to put this code into an already existing data-bound field.

Generally, a component is better when you want to create something to work by itself; if you are simply adding visual changes and behavior to an already existing component, the best way is to use a binding handler.

This new binding handler should manage the functionality of clearing the field, and a way to know whether the icon should be shown; it should also add a template HTML into the View, just after the bound element.

The template system of KnockoutJS manages two kinds of templates:

- Named template (using a script tag with an ID)
- Anonymous template (the children of a DOM element are the template)

We could simply put in the document the template we want to use, or maybe we could extend the template system by adding another kind of template:

- String-based (a string from the View Model will be used for the template)

To implement this new kind of template, we create a new file, BookingOnline/app/stringTemplateEngine.js, with the following code:

```
define(["knockout"], function(ko) {
  //private template source that is simply a string
  var StringTemplateSource = function(template) {
    this.template = template;
  };

  StringTemplateSource.prototype.text = function() {
    return this.template;
  };

  var stringTemplateEngine = new ko.nativeTemplateEngine();
  stringTemplateEngine.makeTemplateSource = function(template) {
    return new StringTemplateSource(template);
  };

  return stringTemplateEngine;
});
```

This code creates a new TemplateEngine starting from the ko.nativeTemplateEngine, updating it to use as source the template string itself (encapsulated into a stringTemplateSource function).

Now we can use this module easily; we just need to tell KnockoutJS that we want to render a template using this engine; look at how we can do so, creating a new source file named `BookingOnline/app/binding-handler/clearable.js` with this content:

```
define(function(require) {
  var ko = require("knockout"),
      $ = require("jquery"),
      stringTemplateEngine = require("stringTemplateEngine"),
      template = require("text!./clearable.html");
```

Here, we are requiring the template engine, and defining the template we want to use; if you see, we are loading the HTML from an external template to follow the MVVM pattern. Let's see the markup for the template (`clearable.html`):

```
<span data-bind="visible:isNotEmpty, click: clear">
  <i class="ui-icon ui-icon-circle-close"> </i>
</span>
```

As you can see, it's almost the same as the markup we used before for the icon, but here we are not using any specific observable name because we are going to inject the function inside the binding context.

Now, we can continue with the binding handler:

```
ko.bindingHandlers.clearable = {
  init: function(element, valueAccessor) {
    var value = valueAccessor(),
        bindingContext = {
          clear: function() {
            value(undefined);
          },
          isNotEmpty: ko.computed(function() {
            return this();
          }, value)
        },
        options = {
          templateEngine: stringTemplateEngine
        },
```

```
        span = document.createElement("SPAN");

    $(element).after(span);
    ko.renderTemplate(template, bindingContext, options, span,
"replaceNode");
      }
    };
  });
```

The binding handler `clearable` creates `bindingContext` with the two functions we used before: `clear` and `isNotEmpty`; both functions use the observable from the parameters.

Here, you can see how we can tell which template engine to choose (the third parameter of `ko.renderTemplate`). Then, we create the span element as a sibling of the current element, and apply the template inside that node, replacing the node.

Now we can use this binding handler inside our components, so update the View Model, `search.js`, adding this row after the block of `require`, in this way:

```
require("binding-handlers/datepicker");
require("binding-handlers/clearable");
```

Then, remove the code we wrote before to manage this functionality for the destination; remove both these rows because we don't need them anymore:

```
this.destination.isNotEmpty = ko.computed(function() { … }, this);
this.destination.clear = function() { … };
```

And finally, add the `data-bind` inside the View (`search.html`); here, there is the full block:

```
    <div>
      <input type="text" placeholder="Enter a destination"
            data-bind="autoComplete: destination,
                      autoCompleteEvents: destination.events,
                      autoCompleteOptions: destination.options,
                      clearable: destination" />
      <label> Check In:
        <input type="text" readonly
              data-bind="datepicker: checkIn,
                        clearable: checkIn" /> </label>
      <label> Check Out:
```

```
<input type="text" readonly
        data-bind="datepicker: checkOut,
                   clearable: checkOut" /> </label>
    <input type="submit" data-bind="enable: isValid" />
</div>
```

And now, all clearable fields are ready.

Making the button easy to customize

We should spend a bit of time on the search button as well.

This binding handler for the button is the easiest realized till now, so I'm leaving this as an exercise for you; try to realize it, and, as the last resort, use the following explanation to check.

Create a binding handler named BookingOnline/app/binding-handler/button.js with this code:

```
define(function(require) {
  var ko = require("knockout"),
      $ = require("jquery"),
      button = require("ui/button");

  ko.bindingHandlers.button = {
    init: function (element, valueAccessor) {
      button({}, element);

      ko.utils.domNodeDisposal.addDisposeCallback(element,
        function() {
          $(element).button("destroy");
        }
      );
    }
  };
});
```

Here, we are just applying the jQuery Button Widget to the element, and then we will manage the release of the resource when the button gets disposed.

Then, we will update the View Model, `search.js`, adding the require code inside the `require` block, in this way:

```
require("binding-handlers/clearable");
require("binding-handlers/button");
```

And, as the last step we will update the View, `search.html`, modifying the button code into this one:

```
<input type="submit" data-bind="button: true,
                                enable: isValid" />
```

The component is now (almost) ready.

Communicating with other components

We realized the form, and now the customer can search for hotels; clicking on the search button will send a request to the backend, and we will use the result inside other components.

We need a way to enable communication between components without the need for direct referencing each other.

In the next chapter, we will look at the concept of Publish/Subscribe, but now we will go with a simple **Event Manager** module (following the Mediator design pattern).

When you got the files for the communication with the backend, you download `BookingOnline/app/services/eventManager.js`.

This module exposes three functions:

- `function on (event name, callback)`: use it to listen for named event
- `function off (event name, callback)`: use it to stop current listening for a named event
- `function trigger (event name, parameters)`: use it to send a message to the listeners

If you check the `rest.js` module, you will find there a function named `getHotelByDestination`. At the end of the function you will see that it uses the `eventManager` module to trigger an event named `search:result` with the results of the last search.

We can use it to get the results inside the other modules. And, best of all, we can just call it inside our Search Form button event, to finally finish this component.

Update in `search.js` the function `execute` in this way:

```
Search.prototype.execute = function() {
  rest.getHotelByDestination(this.destination());
};
```

And voila, the component is done.

Adding the Hotel Cards

Now we can develop the Hotel Cards.

As you can see in this wireframe, this component is almost self-contained, so it's normal to realize it with another component.

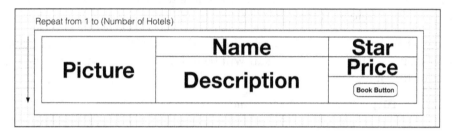

This component will be much shorter than the previous one because we are not going to put too much effort into it; the main reason is that we get the information to show from the backend, and we just draw it here.

The hardest part here is the HTML and the CSS behind, but we are not so interested in such code in this case.

As the first step, we will create the View Model of this new component, putting this code in `BookingOnline/app/components/hotelCard.js`:

```
define(function(require) {
  var ko = require("knockout"),
      template = require("text!./hotelCard.html");
  require("binding-handlers/button");
```

We will use the `button` binding handler to improve the style of our Booking buttons:

```
function HotelCard(data) {
  ko.utils.extend(this, data);
```

We will then extend this object with the data we get from the parameters; we don't need any observable here because there is no dynamicity here:

```
this.getThumb = function() {
  return this.image || "/images/default.jpg";
};
```

We will now define a function (getThumb) to get the image to show, taking the default image if the hotel doesn't have one:

```
this.starRange = ko.utils.range(1, this.stars);
var colors = ['bad', 'normal', 'normal', 'good', 'good'];
this.starType = colors[this.stars - 1];
}
```

These last three rows are used for a nice effect, like the one you find inside the tutorial section of KnockoutJS: *show stars*.

Here, we get an array to use with a foreach binding handler, and a kind of star color depending on the number: a single star will be red, two or three stars will be yellow, and four or five stars will be green:

```
HotelCard.prototype.book = function() {};

  return {viewModel: HotelCard, template: template};
});
```

We will put the remaining code to manage the click of the booking button, and then return the structure required from KnockoutJS to use a component.

Easy, isn't it?

The code of the View (hotelCard.html) is easy too; you can see there is more structure and code for styling than markup we are interested in:

```
<img class="hotel-left" data-bind="attr: { src: getThumb() }">
<div class="hotel-center">
  <div class="hotel-name" data-bind="text: hotel"></div>
  <div class="hotel-description"
       data-bind="html: description"></div>
</div>
<div class="hotel-right">
  <div class="hotel-star">
```

```
<!-- ko foreach: starRange -->
  <span class="stars"
        data-bind="css: $parent.starType"></span>
<!-- /ko -->
</div>
<div class="hotel-price" data-bind="text: price"></div>
<div class="hotel-book">
 <input type="button" value="Book"
        data-bind="button: true, click: book"/>
</div>
</div>
```

Here, we are showing an image choosing the attribute source from the function we defined before; then the name of the hotel; the description; and a number of span equals to the number of stars, displaying a star for each of them.

Then we show the price and we apply the `button` binding handler to the booking button.

Interesting here is the usage of the `html` binding handler for the description; we use it because our text is full of HTML tags; it's not a bad choice, but remember all the time that you have to check all the data you will show there to avoid a security hole.

As the last step, we will update our main View to use this new component. Update the View, `index.html`, putting this code just after the other component (in this way):

```
<div data-bind="component: 'search'"></div>
<div class="hotels">
<!-- ko foreach: hotels -->
  <div class="hotel-card"
       data-bind="component: { name: 'hotel-card',
                               params: $data }"></div>
<!-- /ko -->
</div>
```

Here, we are using the component as we have done before, but we pass as parameter the current item of the array; this is the reason we find the item inside the `data` parameter in the constructor of the Hotel Card.

Now we will fill the `hotels` observable inside the View Model, `index.js`; add a reference to the Event Manager (in this way):

```
var $ = require("jquery"),
    ko = require("knockout"),
    eventManager = require("services/eventManager"),
    viewModel = {};
```

Then, update the View Model property, putting the new observable array:

```
viewModel = {
  hotels: ko.observableArray([])
};
```

As the next step, we will register, to get the list of Hotel Cards, for the event `search:result`:

```
eventManager.on("search:result", function(data) {
  viewModel.hotels(data);
});
```

We use this event to update our list of Hotel Cards.

Last but not least, we will register this component; add this code after the registration of the Search Form:

```
ko.components.register("hotel-card",
                       {require: "components/hotelCard"});
```

If you have done everything till now, and you took the images and the code from the backend, your web application should be similar to this one:

Summary

In this chapter, we have seen all the remaining functionalities of KnockoutJS (core), which we skipped in the previous chapter.

The application we realized was simple enough, but we used it to learn better how to use components and custom binding handlers.

If you think we put too much code for such a small project, try to think what differences you have seen between the first and the second component: the more component and binding handler code you write, the less you will have to write in the future.

The most important point about components and custom binding handlers is that you have to realize them looking at future reuse; the more good code you write, the better it will be for you later.

The core point of this chapter was AMD and RequireJS; how to use them inside a KnockoutJS project, and why you should do it.

In the next chapter, we will look at how to realize a full-featured SPA with the help of DurandalJS, a framework built around jQuery, KnockoutJS, and RequireJS.

3
SPA for Timesheet Management

In this chapter, we will realize a full-featured SPA for a shifts-based working company.

We will create a login form to give access to two different kinds of people: workers and team managers; we give them a dashboard to check the status of the days, and a grid to manage rest days, holiday assignation, and time-related tasks.

By the end of this chapter, you'll know:

- What is an SPA, which kind of libraries/frameworks we can use to realize an SPA, and how to choose between them.
- What is DurandalJS, and how can we use it for our project.
- How to use the hash mark to create an improved navigation experience with multiple routes.
- How to realize dashboards and grids (with sorting, paging, and asynchronous data loading).

Let's start with the project.

Analysing the project briefly – Timesheet SPA

A few years ago, I was working as a consultant for the biggest flying company in my country; the main project I worked on was the time management system for the workers.

These kinds of applications are built for two different kinds of customers:

- **Employees**: These are the people working inside a team; they work inside a shift-based time system to cover the whole day (or a big part of it), they need a system to manage permission, holiday, rest days, and to submit requests to change shifts with other employees.

- **Team managers**: They have many people working for them, and their job is to manage all the shifts; they need a system to monitor the shifts of each day, and a way to accept/reject requests from their subordinates.

In this kind of system, we have many business rules to respect, such as the minimum hours between two turns, and how many consecutive days can be worked before a rest.

The application we want to realize in this chapter will ask the user to login, and then it will show a dashboard to check the shifts, functionalities to ask permission, free days, and a way for the Team Manager to accept or reject them.

And we will do all of this with an SPA.

The SPA feature for the Timesheet SPA

A Single Page Application is a web application realized with a single page, giving to the end user the experience of a desktop application.

In an SPA, when the user lands inside the application, the HTML, CSS, and JavaScript of the main layout get downloaded; then, with the help of Ajax, the internal view is loaded based on the state of the application and the user actions within the structure of the main layout.

Good SPA uses hash fragment (or the new HTML5 API `pushState`/`replaceState`) inside the URL to give the user a way to navigate between pages keeping browser history, using the back and forward button of the browser, and to bookmark the URL to come back later to the current page.

In an SPA, the concept of a page derives from the current status of the system; the user expects that different URLs give different pages, and we normally achieve this with the help of a client routing manager.

Two important points to remember when you realize an SPA are the memory usage and the performances.

After an SPA is loaded, the JavaScript and page will keep running until the user navigates to other sites; for this reason, you must check you are not leaking memory, and that your components are clean after their destruction. You have to do a lot of performance tests (a load test can help here).

Choosing the right tool for the project

We already built an SPA in the previous chapter.

The `component` feature of KnockoutJS gives us a way to make SPA, because we can put components inside a page, and with the help of control flow binding we can load and update the view without any page reload.

The main problem with this solution is the maintainability of the application.

You can easily see that it should be really hard to build and manage a big complex application in this way.

At the start of 2014, Steven Sanderson (main maintainer of KnockoutJS) started a conversation with the team about the new features component and custom element.

Steven Sanderson explained that these new features were not intended to move KnockoutJS into a fully featured SPA framework because the main goal of this library is doing data-binding, and it is doing it really well.

For this reason, if you are going to realize an SPA it's better to use a framework built for that, instead of relying only on KnockoutJS.

You can find the conversation at `https://github.com/knockout/knockout/issues/1273`.

If you looked around for an SPA framework, you probably already heard about Angular, Backbone, and Ember.

Another important SPA framework you can find, based on KnockoutJS, is **DurandalJS**.

One of the most important features of DurandalJS (`http://durandaljs.com/`) is that it is a framework built over jQuery, KnockoutJS, and RequireJS.

This means you can reuse all the knowledge you have of these three libraries, and you can have an SPA with the same features of the others frameworks.

 Maybe you never heard about DurandalJS, but just to understand the importance of this library, the creator of this framework is now working together with the team behind Angular to put all the best features of those two frameworks into what will be Angular 2.0.

Choosing between DurandalJS or plain KnockoutJS

If you are unsure about choosing DurandalJS instead of plain KnockoutJS for an SPA, let's look at what DurandalJS can give us:

- A client router to manage navigation, screen state, and full history support
- Full control of application lifecycle with a point of extendibility
- Great composition system with full support of asynchronous loading of the components
- Integrated event management
- Message boxes (modal or not), using jQuery
- Easy testability for each module and for the whole application

Other than this, it suggests a convention over configuration strategy, so you can start using it easily, as you will see in a few moments.

The main difference between DurandalJS and KnockoutJS is the goal of each one: KnockoutJS is a data-binding library while DurandalJS is an SPA framework.

In Timesheet SPA project, we want to provide various views depending on the role and on the state of the application, so it should be good to have a client router.

A nice way to show the forms for the requests is within a modal message box, which is also included in DurandalJS.

For all these reasons we are going to use it for this web application (and also for the SPA we will build in *Chapter 5, Wizard for the Public Administration*).

 DurandalJS was built before KnockoutJS 3.2, so it uses its own version of compositions; when you use the latest version of both libraries you can use the component of KnockoutJS as you have seen or the widget of DurandalJS as you prefer.

For this chapter, we will loosely follow the *Getting started* guide we find on the DurandalJS website at `http://www.durandaljs.com/get-started.html`.

Creating a new project starting with the HTML StarterKit

As the first step, we download the `HTML StarterKit` file from the DurandalJS website (we are going to use DurandalJS 2.1).Then we put all the content of the `HTML StarterKit.zip` file into a new folder named `TimesheetSPA` to be the root of our project.

Let's look at the folder structure of our starting project:

- Inside the root folder you find `index.html`, the starting point of the whole application

- The two other files here (`Changes.txt`, `README.md`) are useless for us, so you can remove them

- Inside the folder `lib` you find the following libraries: **jQuery** (1.9.1), **KnockoutJS** (3.1), **RequireJS** (2.1.11), **Font-Awesome** 4.0.3, and **Bootstrap** (3.1.1)

- You already know the first three libraries, but as you can see we are not using the latest version of them; replace the current libraries with the latest one we used in the previous chapter (jQuery 1.11.1 and KnockoutJS 3.2); this requires an update in `app/main.js`, which we will see in detail later

 The main reason to update the libraries is that each new version takes with it many new features, and many bug fixes; you should look at the change log between different versions before updating, but normally it's safe to update between different minor versions.

- Font-Awesome is a really nice library of icons, not required from DurandalJS but nice to have; you can see how the project uses it inside the `shell.html` file, with this row:

```
<i class="fa fa-spinner fa-spin fa-2x"></i>
```

- Bootstrap is a framework to develop responsive, mobile first projects

- Inside `app` you find all the code used for the application

- `app/main.js` is the starting point used from `index.html` with RequireJS; you find there the configuration of RequireJS, then the code to configure DurandalJS and to set `viewmodels/shell` as **root view model**

> The root view model represents the main View Model (and the related View) of the application; if you think in the same way as KnockoutJS, you can consider this the `$root` View Model used to start the binding inside the page.
>
> You can pass a third parameter inside the call to the `setRoot` function, to indicate which is the DOM item to use for the binding, or it will default to `#applicationHost`.

- `app/viewmodels/shell.js` and `app/views/shell.html` define the layout of the page, and uses the client router to define which module to show depending on the current URL

- Inside `app/viewmodels` you find all the View Model already created for this application, and inside `app/views` you find the associated View

> The view is automatically located by convention (you defined to use them with this code inside `main.js`: `viewLocator.useConvention();`) by replacing the `viewmodels` folder path with `views`. So the only requirement is that you give your `views` and `viewmodels` the same name.

DurandalJS puts the configuration of RequireJS inside the `app/main.js` file, and you have to update it to point to the right name of the libraries; update the following rows:

```
'knockout': "../lib/knockout/knockout-3.1.0",
'bootstrap': "../lib/bootstrap/js/bootstrap",
'jquery': "../lib/jquery/jquery-1.9.1"
```

Into:

```
'knockout': "../lib/knockout/knockout-3.2.0",
'bootstrap': "../lib/bootstrap/js/bootstrap",
'jquery': "../lib/jquery/jquery-1.11.2.min"
```

Here I'm assuming you put the jquery-1.11.2.min.js file inside the folder lib/jquery file and knockout-3.2.0.js inside lib/knockout.

 RequireJS configuration uses the path **as-is**, adding .js at the end of the name; so, you can use any file naming you like, just remember to put the full path there with only the trailing .js removed

Building Timesheet SPA with DurandalJS

Now that we have seen which tool we can use, we can start analyzing the project and how we can build it with DurandalJS.

Before looking at the routes and the components we should update the loading text we get when we load the application.

Update index.html, changing the title from Durandal to Timesheet SPA, and the message from Durandal Starter Kit to Timesheet SPA.

Then update main.js, changing the app.title value into Timesheet SPA.

Now the title of the starting page will be Welcome | Timesheet SPA.

Components of this project

To build an SPA, we have to decide which routes we will use and what we serve for each route.

Let's list the routes with a short description:

- /: This is the main page for the Employee.
- /login: This is the login page.
- /team: This is the main page for the Team Manager

We update app/viewmodels/shell.js to put these routes; substitute the activate function into this one:

```
activate: function() {
  router.map([
    {route: "", title: "User Dashboard",
     moduleId: "viewmodels/employee", authType: "employee"},
    {route: "login", title: "Login",
     moduleId: "viewmodels/login"},
    {route: "manager", title: "Team Manager Dashboard",
     moduleId: "viewmodels/manager", authType: "manager"}
  ]).buildNavigationModel();
  return router.activate();
}
```

For each route we use hash for the URL, the title, the moduleId, and the field authType, which we will use later to check if the logged user can see and use that route.

Here we added a custom field named authType, because we want to discriminate between different routes and user types; you can add additional parameters to the routes, if you think you need them.

Now, when we start the application, the router will try to load the View Model app/viewmodels/employee.js, and its View app/views/employee.html.

You can remove the old modules (welcome.js, welcome.html, flickr.js, flickr.html, and detail.html) because now there are no routes pointing to them.

Let's create the new View Models and the new Views; put this boilerplate code for the View Models (employee.js, login.js, and manager.js inside app/viewmodels/):

```
define(function(require) {
  var ko = require("knockout");

  function Ctor() {};

  return Ctor;
});
```

With this code DurandalJS will find each View Model and you avoid getting error messages.

> When you write a module you can return an object or a constructor function; if you return an object it will be shared (so, it will be a Singleton); if you return a function the requiring code could use it to instantiate new objects of that class.
>
> DurandalJS uses the same logic inside the composition logic: if you compose a module with a constructor function (like the boilerplate code we wrote) it will initialize a new object each time.
>
> So, if your module represents a day with its data, you should use a function; you should return an object if you are representing the data of the logged user (single instance in all the web applications).

For the boilerplate code of the Views (`employee.html`, `login.html`, and `manager.html` inside `app/views/`) you can create an empty file with only this markup:

```
<section></section>
```

Getting the code for the Client-Server interface

For this project, we need to get data from the backend; KnockoutJS is a pure frontend library, so the development of the code for the server side would be really out of the scope of this book.

For this reason, I put all the code for the interaction with the server into `app/services/rest.js`, like you have seen in the *Chapter 2, Starting Small and Growing in a Modular Way*.

Inside the `server` folder, I have put all the additional data (such as JSON and image) that you get using `rest.js`.

If you check the `server/users.json` file, you can find all the users and passwords that you can use to login to the system we are going to realize.

So, before going on, get the `StartingPackage.zip` file for this chapter from the Packt Publishing website and decompress it in the `TimesheetSPA` folder.

Now we can start with the development, and we start it with the first component.

Checking authentication – Login component

The first module we build is the Login component.

We use it to send the credentials to the backend, to check if the user is authenticated, and which module it should use.

This module will be a simple form with two fields: user ID and password.

 An internal project for big companies normally doesn't need any registration form; people with permission to use it are already registered into DB/LDAP, and we can just use these data; this is the reason we are not realizing any registration form; you can find one in *Chapter 5, Wizard for the Public Administration*.

Let's look at a wireframe of the Login View:

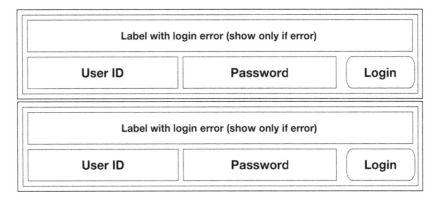

Put these rows into the `login.html` View:

```
<section>
  <p data-bind="text: error"></p>
  <form data-bind="submit: login">
    <input type="text" placeholder="User ID"
           data-bind="textInput: userId" />
    <input type="password" placeholder="Password"
           data-bind="textInput: password" />
    <input type="submit" value="Login"
           data-bind="enable: canLogin" />
  </form>
</section>
```

We put a paragraph to show error messages (text:error), if present.

Then we have a form with the two fields for userId and password; we use the textInput data binding to get continuous update for the canLogin computed observable.

If you have text for userId and password the button gets enabled, and if you submit the form, it executes the login function.

The code for the View Model (login.js) is simple too:

```
define(function(require) {
  var ko = require("knockout"),
      rest = require("services/rest"),
      router = require("plugins/router");

  function Ctor() {
    this.userId = ko.observable();
    this.password = ko.observable();
    this.error = ko.observable();
    this.canLogin = ko.computed(function() {
      return this.userId() && this.password();
    }, this);
  };
```

Here we use KnockoutJS, a reference to our backend interface, and a reference to the router; we need it to navigate to the other pages in a clean way.

Then we define the observable properties we used inside the View:

```
  Ctor.prototype.login = function() {
    var result = rest.login(this.userId(), this.password());
    this.error(result.error);

    var options = {replace: true , trigger: true};
    if (rest.isEmployee()) {
      router.navigate("", options);
    } else if (rest.isTeamManager()) {
      router.navigate("manager", options);
    }
  };

  return Ctor;
});
```

We start by trying to login; then we update the error text with the error message (or undefined if there is no error).

If we authenticate, we look for the type of user, and navigate to that page.

The first parameter for the function is the hash to navigate to.

The second parameter is an option object; in this case, we ask DurandalJS to replace the current hash inside the browser history with the next (so it will remove the `#login` tag from the browser history), and to trigger the page change (otherwise it changes only the URL inside the browser).

 The user expects a fluid navigation inside the application; you should remove all the hash we need only for the process; remember to remove all the useless steps.

Now if you navigate to /`#login` you get the Login page; you can try to login with the user ID and password you find inside `server/users.js`.

If you log in as an Employee, you get redirected to / and if you log in as a Team Manager you get redirected to /`manager`.

Auto-redirecting navigation to Login page

Actually, we miss two features to complete this page:

- A guard for authenticated-only page
- A logout button

There is a function of the router plugin you can use to implement the first feature: `router.guardRoute`.

This function gets called each time there is a navigation step, and you can use it to prevent navigation or to override the route.

Add the function `guardRoute` to `shell.js` in this way:

```
activate: function() {
  router.guardRoute = function(instance, instruction) {
    if (!rest.isAuthenticated() &&
        instruction.config.moduleId !== "viewmodels/login") {
      return "login";
```

```
    } else if (rest.isEmployee() &&
            instruction.config.authType !== "employee") {
        return "";
    } else if (rest.isTeamManager() &&
            instruction.config.authType !== "manager") {
        return "manager";
    }
    return true;
};
router.map([
```

Here we check for three different conditions:

- If user is not authenticated and we are not going to the login page we navigate there
- If the user is an employee he can navigate only to the page for employees
- If the user is a manager he can navigate only to the page for managers

There is no mention of this method inside the documentation of DurandalJS; but you can find this information inside the source of the plugin `router.js`.

`guardRoute` can return a Boolean, a string, or a promise:

- A Boolean determines whether the route should activate or be cancelled
- A string causes a redirect to the specified route
- It can also be a promise for either of these value types

Then update the dependencies of this module, adding `rest.js` under `services` and Knockout:

```
define(["plugins/router", "knockout", "services/rest"],
    function (router, ko, rest) {
```

With this code, we have now protected the pages from being accessed by an un-authenticated user.

Adding a logout button

We will put the button into the top bar, so we have to modify the Shell module.

Add these functions to the returning object inside `shell.js`:

```
canLogout: function() {
  var activeInstruction = router.activeInstruction();
  return activeInstruction &&
         activeInstruction.fragment !== "login";
},
logout: function() {
  rest.logout();
  router.navigate("login");
},
```

The first function is there because we want to show the button only if the user is authenticated (and we put a guard to be sure that un-authenticated user will be redirected to #login).

The second one executes the logout and then navigates to the login page.

We are going to update the `shell.html` View, so it's a good time to clean the interface.

Substitute the whole block:

```
<form class="navbar-form navbar-right" role="search" ...>...</form>
```

With:

```
<div class="navbar-form navbar-right"
     data-bind="visible: canLogout()">
  <button data-bind="click: logout">Logout</button>
</div>
```

Here we are using the two previous functions.

And now we have a working login/logout system, so we can continue with the next component.

Making a dashboard for the Employee

Each Employee should have a dashboard with information; for this we need:

- A main section with details of the user
- A section with the shifts for the next three days
- A table with the shifts of the week/month/year (with a button to change the selected view)
- A button for each day inside the table, to request permission for that day
- A button to create a leave request
- A button inside each day having a shift to request a shift change.

The dashboard should be like this:

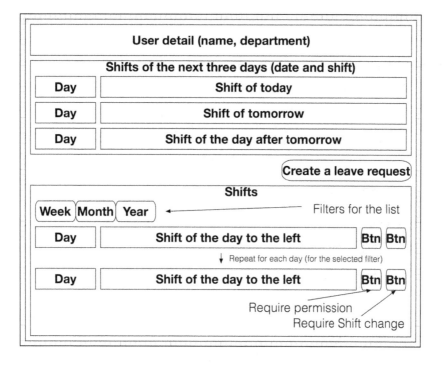

In this dashboard, we have three buttons with an associated modal form; we will look at their wireframe and logic later.

This time we start updating the View, building it block by block; put this markup in employee.html:

```
<section>
  <div>
    User <span data-bind="text: name"></span>
    (ID <span data-bind="text: userId"></span>)
    - Department: <span data-bind="text: department"></span>
  </div>
```

The first block will contain the basic data of the current user; we show the name, the userId, and the department.

We cannot change this data, so we don't need to put all these properties inside an observable.

Here is the initial code for the employee.js View Model:

```
define(function(require) {
  var ko = require("knockout"),
      rest = require("services/rest"),
      helper = require("services/helper"),
      app = require("durandal/app");

  function Employee() {
    var user = rest.user();
    if (!user)
      return;

      var depId = user.departmentId,
        departments = rest.departments(),
        timesheet = rest.timesheet();

    this.name = user.name;
    this.userId = user.userId;
    this.department = departments[depId].department;

    this.timesheet = timesheet[user.id];
  };

  return Employee;
});
```

Here we are giving the View all the fields it needs; we take the data from the `rest` component, and we keep them as normal properties.

The next block to add inside the View is:

```
<div>
  <div>Shifts of the next three days</div>
  <!-- ko foreach: next -->
    <div>
      <span data-bind="text: day" class="w20 inline"></span>
      <span data-bind="component:{name:'shift',params:$data}"
            class="w80 inline"></span>
    </div>
  <!-- /ko -->
</div>
```

Here we show a number of items we find inside the `next` array, and we want to show the `day` and `shift`; at the moment we show only the shift number, but maybe later we will try to improve it; for this reason we build it as a component.

For this component, we create the folder `app/components`; then we put the View of the component, named `shift.html`, with this code:

```
<span data-bind="text: shift"></span>
```

The `shift.js` View Model is simpler than ever:

```
define(function(require) {
    var ko = require("knockout"),
        template = require("text!./shift.html");

    function Shift(data) {
        this.shift = data.shift;
    }

    return {viewModel: Shift, template: template};
});
```

The Shift constructor gets the actual shifts as a parameter, and we store it to use in the View.

Now we go back to the Employee module.

We have to register our new component, so we put this code before the `Employee` (`employee.js`) constructor:

```
ko.components.register("shift", {require: "components/shift"});
```

We must define the `next` property with this code inside the constructor:

```
this.next = helper.getTimesheetByDays(this.timesheet, 3);
```

Here, we delegate to another function (you can find it inside the Helper module), the responsibility to give us the shifts for a number of days; in this way, we can reuse it later for the grid.

Going back to the View, the next block contains only a button, so it's really short and simple:

```
<div>
  <button data-bind="click: createLeaveRequest">
    Create leave request
  </button>
</div>
```

We want to bind the click of the button with a modal dialog with the form; to do this we use a functionality exposed from the `app` module, adding this code to the View Model:

```
Employee.prototype.createLeaveRequest = function() {
  app.showDialog({
    viewUrl: "views/form-leave-request"
  });
};
```

As you can see, we use the `showDialog` function to use the dialog plugin of DurandalJS.

Sometimes you want to display only a View without any View Model related; in this case, you can use a variant of the previous code:

```
app.showDialog({
    viewUrl: "views/form-leave-request"
});
```

You will not find any mention of the parameter `viewUrl` inside the documentation; at the most you can find a reference to this:

```
dialog.MessageBox.setViewUrl("path/to/your/custom/
view")
```

Anyway, the code with the parameter is easier to use, and it's applied just for that use.

We will look later at the code of the modal, because we have to finish the current View.

We can go with the latest block of this View:

```
<div>
  <div>
    <button data-bind="click: showWeek">Week</button>
    <button data-bind="click: showMonth">Month</button>
    <button data-bind="click: showYear">Year</button>
  </div>
```

Here we put three different visualizations of the data inside the grid we are going to define.

The code inside the View Model to bind to them is really simple:

```
Employee.prototype.showWeek = function() {
    this.workDays(helper.getTimesheetByDays(this.timesheet, 7));
};

Employee.prototype.showMonth = function() {
    this.workDays(helper.getTimesheetByDays(this.timesheet, 31));
};

Employee.prototype.showYear = function() {
    this.workDays(helper.getTimesheetByDays(this.timesheet, 365));
};
```

We also put these lines at the end of the constructor to initialize the workDays array:

```
this.workDays = ko.observableArray();
this.showWeek();
```

Now we can put the table for the grid into the View:

```
<table>
  <thead>
    <tr>
      <th class="w20">Day</th>
      <th class="w60">Shift</th>
      <th class="w10"></th><th class="w10"></th>
    </tr>
  </thead>
  <tbody data-bind="foreach: workDays">
    <tr>
      <td data-bind="text: day"></td>
      <td data-bind="component: { name: 'shift',
                                  params: $data }"></td>
      <td><button data-bind="click: $parent.askPermission">
            Permission </button></td>
      <td><button data-bind="click: $parent.askShiftChange">
            Change</button></td>
    </tr>
  </tbody>
</table>
  </div>
</section>
```

This really long piece of code is really simple; we are putting a table, with four columns, and a row for each day inside the workDays array with the name of the day (day), the component for the shift (component: {...}) and two buttons to open two more dialogs (we will look at their code later).

If you look at the markup, you can see I put many w* classes; we can find the definition inside the file starterkit.css (you got from StartingPackage.zip).

We also need to add the two functions (`askPermission`, `askShiftChange`) that we called inside the View to the View Model; add these lines inside the View Model:

```
Employee.prototype.askPermission = function() {
  app.showDialog("viewmodels/form-permission");
};

Employee.prototype.askShiftChange = function() {
  app.showDialog("viewmodels/form-shift-change");

};
```

Transforming a table into a grid with bells and whistles

A great plugin to manage a table with JavaScript is the jQuery plugin named **DataTables** (`http://datatables.net`).

We are going to use the version 1.10.3.

Download it and put the whole folder (`DataTables-1.10.3/media`) inside our project as `TimesheetSPA/lib/datatables`.

Every time you download a new library, you have to perform two steps to get everything working:

1. Update the configuration of RequireJS (inside `app/main.js`).
2. Update the main View (`index.html`) to use the new style sheet you get.

Now add the following line inside the `requirejs.config/paths` object (`main.js`):

```
"datatables" : "../lib/datatables/js/jquery.dataTables.min"
```

Then put a line with this markup inside the `index.html` file:

```
<link rel="stylesheet" href="lib/datatables/css/jquery.dataTables.min.css" />
```

Now we can use the library as a custom binding handler.

As we have done in the previous chapter, create a new folder inside `TimesheetSPA/app` named `binding-handlers`, then create a new file `datatable.js` with the following code:

```
define(function(require) {
    var ko = require("knockout"),
        composition = require("durandal/composition"),
        $ = require("jquery");

    require("datatables");
```

Here, we follow the same pattern we used in the last chapter to create the binding handler using AMD; it's a jQuery plugin, so we simply get it without putting a variable inside.

```
composition.addBindingHandler("dataTable", {
    init: function(element, valueAccessor, allBindingsAccessor) {
```

Here we use a different way to define the binding handler; in a non-DurandalJS project, we should use `ko.bindingHandlers.dataTable`, but here we use a method of `composition`.

DurandalJS expose this method to create delayed binding handler; they execute only after the composition is complete, so you need to use them when you are going to bind with a property of the currently loading module:

```
var value = valueAccessor(),
    allBindings = ko.utils.unwrapObservable(allBindingsAccessor()),
    options = allBindings.dataTableOptions || {},
    $element = $(element);

$element.dataTable(options);

ko.utils.domNodeDisposal.addDisposeCallback(element, function() {
    $element.dataTable().fnDestroy();
});
```

I think you know how this code works, because it is almost the same as the previous custom binding handler:

```
            value.subscribe(function(oldValue) {
                $element.dataTable().fnDestroy();
                $element.find("tbody tr").remove();
            }, null, "beforeChange");

            value.subscribe(function() {
                $element.dataTable(options);
            }, null);
        }
    });
});
```

The main problem with this plugin is that it doesn't give any way to reload the table after a modification of the HTML document.

For this reason, in this implementation, we are going to destroy the `datatable` when the underlying array changes, and rebuild it after.

It's not the best solution, because we are going to recreate the `datatable` each time, but is a simple, easy, and quick way to do it, so it's ok for the sake of simplicity.

If you want to implement it in an optimized way, you can follow the guide you find at `http://datatables.net/dev/knockout/`.

Now we can add the reference to this binding handler inside our View Model `employee.js`; add this row just after the starting `require(...)` lines:

```
require("binding-handlers/datatable");
```

Now we can use it inside the `employee.html` View; update the `table` tag into this:

```
<table data-bind="dataTable: workDays">
```

With this last step, we have a full working reading dashboard; now we can build the forms to send requests to the Team Manager.

Building a few forms to update data

In this dashboard, we have three buttons; we have already written the code to open modal forms.

The first form we will create is the *Create leave request* form; we start with a wireframe of what we should build.

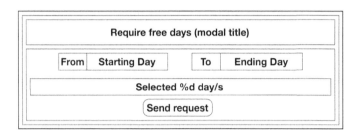

As you can see it's a really simple form; we can build the View (`views/form-leave-request.html`) in a snap:

```html
<div class="modal-content autoclose">
  <div class="modal-header center">
    <h3>Require free days</h3>
  </div>
  <div class="modal-body">
    <form>
      From <input placeholder="Starting Day"
                  data-bind="datepicker: start" />
      To <input placeholder="Ending Day"
                data-bind="datepicker: end" />
      <div class="w100 center">Selected
        <span data-bind="text: numDays"></span> day/s
      </div>
      <div class='center'>
        <button data-bind="click: sendRequest
                           enable: canSend">Send Request</button>
      </div>
    </form>
  </div>
</div>
```

Here we have two fields for the date bound to a `datepicker` binding handler (we got from the `StartingPackage.zip`), a text (`numDay`) with the number of days between `start` and `end`, and a button to send the request (`sendRequest`) to the Team Manager.

To use this binding handler, we have to update the path property inside `main.js` with:

```
"ui": "../lib/jqueryui"
```

Then we go into `index.html` and put the following lines before the link to `css/starterkit.css` to include the style sheets:

```
<link rel="stylesheet" href="css/jqueryui/core.css" />
<link rel="stylesheet" href="css/jqueryui/datepicker.css" />
<link rel="stylesheet" href="css/jqueryui/theme.css" />
```

Now we look at the code for the `viewmodels/form-leave-request.js` View Model:

```
define(function(require) {
  var ko = require("knockout"),
      dialog = require("plugins/dialog"),
      helper = require("services/helper");

  require("binding-handlers/datepicker");
```

We define the module and request the binding handler we want to use and all the dependencies.

Here we require dialog because we will use it to close the modal with a returning value:

```
    function FormFreeDays() {
      this.start = ko.observable();
      this.end = ko.observable();

      this.numDays = ko.computed(function() {
        var start = this.start(), end = this.end();
        return helper.numDaysBetweenDates(end, start);
      }, this);
```

```
    this.canSend = ko.computed(function() {
      return this.start() && this.end() && this.numDays() > 0;
    }, this);
  }
```

Here we define the four properties we bound inside the View; numDay does a simple calculus based on the difference in milliseconds and then it converts to days:

```
    FormFreeDays.prototype.sendRequest = function() {
      dialog.close(this, {
        start: this.start(), end: this.end()
      });
    };


    return FormFreeDays;
  });
```

Look at dialog.close; it closes the modal, then it returns the value to the calling function inside a promise; for this reason, to get these values, we have to update the calling method in this way:

```
    Employee.prototype.createLeaveRequest = function() {
      app.showDialog("viewmodels/form-leave-request")
        .then(function(result) {
          if (result) {
            rest.createLeaveRequest(result);
          }
        }.bind(this));
    };
```

As you can see, we register a callback to app.showDialog, called when the dialog is closed; if the user closes the dialog by clicking outside, the result will be undefined, otherwise we have an object with start and end dates; we send them to our rest service, to send to the backend.

I leave to you as an exercise, the job to build the other two forms; here are the two wireframes to help you.

The *Ask permission* modal form should be like this:

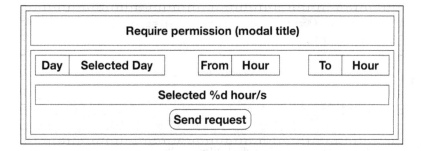

The *Ask shift change* modal form should be similar to this:

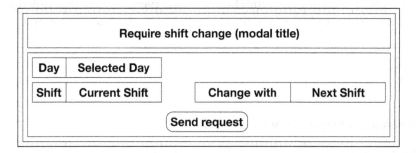

The main differences between these two forms and the previous one is the passage of parameters; let's look at how to do it, then if you want, you can find my code for these forms on the website; or you can do it by yourself as an exercise.

The View Model of the caller is as follows:

```
Employee.prototype.askPermission = function() {
  app.showDialog("viewmodels/form-permission");
};
```

Now, the View Model changes to this:

```
Employee.prototype.askPermission = function(shift, event) {
  app.showDialog("viewmodels/form-permission", this)
    .then(function(result) {
      if (result) {
        rest.requirePermission(result);
      }
    }.bind(this));
};
```

The second parameter is passed to the dialog, as-is.

To get the parameter inside the View Model of the dialog (`form-permission.js`), you have to define the `activate` function; the first parameter of this function will be the parameter you passed from the previous code; let's look at an example:

```
FormShiftChange.prototype.activate = function(shift) {
  this.day = shift.day;
  this.shift = shift.shift;
};
```

Now you can try to realize them by yourself.

With these forms, we have finished all the code for the dashboard for the Employee.

We built a dashboard with all the data acquired from the backend, with a few points of interaction and a grid with paging, sorting, and loading from the server (yes, we skipped the loading from the backend, but you can do it easily if you use the `ajax` and the `data` functions of the `DataTables` plugin).

Now we can go to the Team Manager Dashboard.

Realizing a dashboard for the Team Manager

This dashboard will be really similar to the previous one, so the markup between the two modules will look similar.

Let's look a wireframe of what we want to realize:

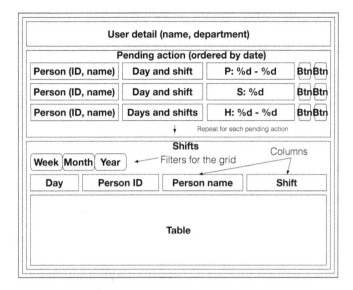

As you can see, the user details should be the same as the previous dashboard.

The next section, about the pending action, will be a grid with some information and two buttons to approve or reject the requests.

Then we have the table with the shifts of each employee, with the same logic of the previous grid.

I'm going to show you the markup for the `manager.html` View; here you show the basic data of the current user:

```
<section>
  <div>
    User <span data-bind="text: name"></span>
    (ID <span data-bind="text: userId"></span>)
    - Department: <span data-bind="text: department"></span>
  </div>
```

This is the markup for the pending actions:

```
<div>
  <div>Pending action</div>
    <table cellspacing="0" width="100%"
           data-bind="dataTable: gridPending">
      <thead>
        <tr>
          <th class="w20">User (ID)</th>
          <th class="w30">Day / Shift</th>
          <th class="w30">Request</th>
          <th class="w10"></th>
          <th class="w10"></th>
        </tr>
      </thead>
      <tbody data-bind="foreach: gridPending">
        <tr>
          <td data-bind="text: user"></td>
          <td data-bind="text: day"></td>
          <td data-bind="text: request"></td>
<td><button data-bind="click: $parent.accept">OK</button></td>
<td><button data-bind="click: $parent.reject">NO</button></td>
        </tr>
      </tbody>
    </table>
  </div>
```

Here you can see we put a markup similar to what we used for the earlier grid; this time we use an observable array named gridPending with the data we need:

```
<div>
  <div>
    <button data-bind="click: showWeek">Week</button>
    <button data-bind="click: showMonth">Month</button>
    <button data-bind="click: showYear">Year</button>
  </div>
  <table data-bind="dataTable: workDays">
    <thead>
      <tr>
        <th class="w20">Day</th>
        <th class="w10">User ID</th>
        <th class="w20">Name</th>
        <th class="w50">Shift</th>
      </tr>
    </thead>
```

```html
<tbody data-bind="foreach: workDays">
  <tr>
    <td data-bind="text: day"></td>
    <td data-bind="text: userId"></td>
    <td data-bind="text: userName"></td>
    <td data-bind="component: { name: 'shift',
                               params: $data }"></td>
  </tr>
</tbody>
</table>
</div>
</section>
```

And here you can see the logic is the same as the previous grid; we put more markup than logic in these grids, right?

In this module, we are going to use the Shift module again; if we try to execute the registration of a component more than once, we get an error; for this reason, we have to move the registration of the components into the main View Model.

For this reason, after the registration of the plugins, move the following line from employee.js to main.js:

```javascript
ko.components.register("shift", {require: "components/shift"});
```

It's ok to move it there because that code is executed before app.start, which is before the execution of the KnockoutJS applyBinding function.

Add KnockoutJS to the dependencies (because we need to register the component):

```javascript
define(["durandal/system", "durandal/app", "durandal/viewLocator",
"knockout"],
        function (system, app, viewLocator, ko) {
```

Now let's look at the source of the new module (manager.js):

```javascript
define(function(require) {
  var ko = require("knockout"),
      rest = require("services/rest");
  require("binding-handlers/datatable");

  function Manager() {
    var user = rest.user(),
        depId = user.departmentId,
        departments = rest.departments(),
        pendingData = rest.getPendingForManager(depId);
```

Here we ask the backend for all the pending data for this manager; almost all the logic of this block is inside the call to getPendingForManager:

```
        this.name = user.name;
        this.userId = user.userId;
        this.depId = depId;
        this.department = departments[depId].department;
        this.gridPending = ko.observableArray(pendingData);
        this.workDays = ko.observableArray();
        this.showWeek();
    }
```

Here we have gridPending and workDays, and we bind both to the datatable binding handler in the View:

```
    Manager.prototype.showWeek = function() {
        this.workDays(rest.getTimesheetForManager(this.depId, 7));
    };

    Manager.prototype.showMonth = function() {
        this.workDays(rest.getTimesheetForManager(this.depId, 31));
    };

    Manager.prototype.showYear = function() {
        this.workDays(rest.getTimesheetForManager(this.depId, 365));
    };
```

Here we ask the backend for the data of all the departments' shifts:

```
    Manager.prototype.accept = function() {
        rest.accept(this);
    };

    Manager.prototype.reject = function() {
        rest.reject(this);
    };

    return Manager;
});
```

As you can see, we are delegating many calls to the back end.

> When you plan the architecture of your web application, try to think about the final users; if they will use it with mainly mobile devices, try to move the weighty business logic inside the server side and leave them to render the results; otherwise, you can move most of the logic (but remember the security concern) to the client side to help with scalability.

Summary

In this chapter, we built a Single Page Application with DurandalJS.

We have seen how to realize an SPA easy to maintain, with all the features of KnockoutJS, and with the usage of a new external library (DataTables).

Now you can build a small-to-large application without adding too much complexity, because all the logic is encapsulated into the Models/View Models, which are testable.

We left out a few interesting points about testability and optimization of the sources, but we will cover them in *Chapter 5, Wizard for the Public Administration*, when we will realize another SPA with DurandalJS.

In the next chapter, we will realize an application to manage money, which is fully integrated with mobile devices using **PhoneGap**, to see what we can get from touch screen devices with the contact list and other additional capabilities.

4
Tracking Expense Using PhoneGap

In the previous chapter, we built a full SPA using the framework DurandalJS.

In this chapter, we will realize a hybrid mobile application to track expenses and plan and manage the budget.

At the end of this chapter, you'll know:

- What a hybrid mobile application is and which kind of frameworks we can use to make one
- What PhoneGap (or Cordova) is, how to install it, and which benefits it can give us
- How to integrate KnockoutJS with jQuery Mobile for this application
- How to get the most from the user environment: using the contacts to get the data for the application
- What kind of test to perform with these kinds of applications

Understanding hybrid mobile applications

Every time you want to build a mobile application you can choose between three kinds of development options:

- Native
- Pure HTML 5
- Hybrid

Each of them has pros and cons and you can find many comparative tables on the Web.

The main reason we are going to create a hybrid application instead of a pure HTML 5 application is that we want to access device features (such as contacts and calendars) and we cannot do it with a pure HTML 5 mobile application.

 You can search for *hybrid mobile application* on Google to get all the explanation you need; I'll not cover more here because it's really out of topic.

The most popular frameworks to realize hybrid mobile applications are:

- Titanium (`http://www.appcelerator.com/titanium/`)
- PhoneGap/Cordova (`http://phonegap.com`)

If you are a BackboneJS developer you should choose Titanium, because they integrate really well using Alloy.

Otherwise you should go to PhoneGap.

There are many different popular frameworks used with PhoneGap, such as:

- **Ionic** (deeply integrated with Angular)
- **Sencha Touch** (from the same company as ExtJS)
- **Bootstrap** (a widely used responsive web framework)
- **jQuery Mobile** (a touch-optimized web framework)

For our application, we skip the first two (because they are not easy to integrate with KnockoutJS), so we have to decide between the last two.

We already have seen Bootstrap in the previous project, with DurandalJS.

A big difference between these two frameworks is that jQuery Mobile has an Ajax-based internal routing system and Bootstrap doesn't have anything like this.

So, for this application, we are going to use jQuery Mobile with PhoneGap.

 It's just an arbitrary decision here, because you could take Bootstrap, a client-side router like `pager.js` (`http://pagerjs.com`) or `Crossroads.js` (`http://millermedeiros.github.com/crossroads.js/`) and you could build almost the same application.

Getting PhoneGap/Cordova

To start using this framework, follow this guide: `http://cordova.apache.org/ docs/en/4.0.0/guide_cli_index.md.html#The%20Command-Line%20Interface_ installing_the_cordova_cli`

> PhoneGap and Cordova are two different names for the same framework; in October 2011 PhoneGap was donated to Apache under the name of Apache Cordova; for this reason, you may find references to both names, but the framework is the same.

During the development, we will use the command-line interface.

We could, ourselves, build the application to be distributed, but we will take advantage of the Adobe PhoneGap Build system; you can use it for free, for any open source application and for private applications you want to build.

To get Cordova working, you need to install NodeJS and a Git client; then, after installing Cordova, we use it to create our new application with this command (from the command line):

```
cordova create PiggyBank com.ko_blueprint.piggybank "Piggy Bank"
```

Cordova will create a new project inside the `PiggyBank` folder, with all the code needed to start.

The easiest way to test the application without a device is with the `browser` platform; this is a fake platform to execute the application inside the browser.

You get it with these commands:

```
cd PiggyBank
cordova platform add browser
```

Now when you want to look at your application you can use this command:

```
cordova run browser
```

This command will copy the modified assets inside the www folder at platforms/browser and will open a browser for the index.html file at platforms/browser/www.

> If you want to integrate the auto-reload behavior into your workflow, you can use the command:
>
> **cordova prepare browser**
>
> It updates the files without opening any browser.
>
> If you use Chrome, you may get an error because it cannot read a local file; you can solve this problem easily — close the browser, then execute:
>
> **cordova run browser**
>
> In this way, it will open the browser again, using a flag (--allow-file-access-from-files) that fixes the problem.

Defining what Piggy Bank should be

The main goal of this application is the management of the budget.

With an easy-to-use interface, the user should configure the account he wants to manage, the details for each transaction he puts inside, and the budget goal based on categories.

We could expand this application with many server-side additions, such as the direct download of information from the bank account, or the synchronization of the data with the family (in this case, we need an authentication system).

To keep the project easy and make it doable within one chapter, we have to decide which features will be mandatory for our **Minimum Viable Product (MVP)**.

> MVP is defined as the product with only those core features that allow the product to be deployed, and no more.

This is the list of the features we need for our MVP:

- The application is for a single user
- A user can create many accounts
- A user puts information about each transaction by hand
- A transaction is represented with a date, an account, a subject, one tag, a textual description, and an amount of money

- There is no currency management; every transaction will be made in dollars

- A user can get a list of all accounts, all categories, and all transactions; he can also get a filtered list of transactions depending on the account or the category

- A user can create, update, and remove any transaction

- For each tag, the user can put as much money as he would use in a defined interval (days, weeks, months, or years)

Creating a starting environment for the project

In the previous chapter, I built a wireframe of each View before the real code, to have an idea of what we were going to build.

I'll do the same here, but before going directly to the code, it's better to prepare our workspace.

We already created the starting structure of the application. Cordova built many folders for us with all the starting code. The main folder of the project is www. You write your code inside that folder, because it's the container of our assets.

When you are ready to build the application to test inside the device, ask Cordova to build the application with the command:

```
cordova build
```

This will create an application package for each platform you added to the project inside the folders platforms/PLATFORM_NAME/build/.

We already decided which frameworks we are going to use, so we can start to put each library inside the www folder.

Make a folder named lib inside the www folder, then download the following libraries inside it:

- jQuery (1.11.1): www/lib/jquery/jquery-1.11.1.min.js

- KnockoutJS (3.2.0): www/lib/knockout/knockout-3.2.0.js

- RequireJS (2.1.15): www/lib/require/require.js

Then download jQuery Mobile (1.4.4): jquery.mobile-1.4.4.zip.

You'll get a ZIP file with much more files than we need; copy the following files/folders into a new folder named `www/lib/jquery-mobile`:

- `jquery.mobile-1.4.4.min.js`
- `jquery.mobile-1.4.4.min.css`
- `images/`

Now we have all the needed libraries to begin our mobile application.

It's really easier to develop the application with a well-organized folder structure, so we try to replicate the logic we have seen in the previous chapter with DurandalJS.

Create the following folders:

- `www/app`
- `www/app/viewmodels`
- `www/app/views`

Then get the `StartingPackage.zip` file for this chapter from the Packt Publishing website and decompress it inside the `www` folder.

Remove the original `www/css/index.css` file (because we got all the styles for the whole application with the Starting Package).

As the last step, remove `www/js/index.js` and then remove the folder `www/js`.

Building the application with jQuery Mobile

From the specification, we have four kinds of entities:

- **Accounts**
- **Categories**
- **Customers**
- **Transactions**

We will track all of them inside a database, and our interface will be a simple CRUD for these entities.

Create, read, update, and delete (CRUD) is the basic operation you can perform with an entity of a persistent storage (such as the WebSQL we use with Cordova).

Speaking about CRUD and user interface, you should build the interface to create new items, to list them all, to look through the detail of a single item, to modify and save the changes, and finally, to delete them.

For this reason, this will be the layout of this application:

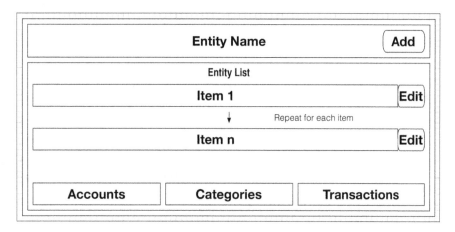

We put a few buttons in the footer to give the user a way to navigate between entities' pages.

In this layout, I excluded the customer view because we will use this application with a mobile device, with a real small resolution, so we cannot put too much text in the header/footer.

In this chapter, we will build only the Account entity, and then we will see what you need to add the others entities, because the code for each of them is really similar, so it should be useless to put all of them here.

Realizing the global layout of the application

Before going to the single pages let's look how to realize the previous generic layout.

We will use the index page to render the basic layout, and then with the help of RequireJS we will load a specific page (with the header and the page content) and apply KnockoutJS to that page.

The main reason we cannot simply put all the script inside each page is that we are going to use the Ajax navigation system of jQuery Mobile, so it will load only the content of the page, skipping all the headers of each new page loaded.

This means that we can put the full page inside `index.html`, and then we put only the page content inside the other Views.

This is the code you should put inside `index.html`:

```
<!DOCTYPE html>
<html>
<head>
  <meta charset="utf-8" />
  <meta name="format-detection" content="telephone=no" />
  <meta name="msapplication-tap-highlight" content="no" />
  <meta name="viewport" content="user-scalable=no, initial-scale=1,
maximum-scale=1, minimum-scale=1, width=device-width, height=device-
height, target-densitydpi=device-dpi" />
  <link href="lib/jquery-mobile/jquery.mobile-1.4.4.min.css"
        rel="stylesheet" type="text/css" />
  <link href="css/styles.css"
        rel="stylesheet" type="text/css" />
  <title>Piggy Bank</title>
</head>
<body>
  <div data-role="header" data-position="fixed" data-theme="a">
    <h1>Piggy Bank</h1>
  </div>

  <div data-role="page"></div>

  <div data-role="footer" data-position="fixed" data-theme="a">
    <div data-role="navbar">
      <ul>
        <li><a data-prefetch="true" data-transition="flip"
```

```
            href="app/views/accounts.html">Accounts</a></li>
        <li><a data-prefetch="true" data-transition="flip"
            href="app/views/categories.html">Categories</a></li>
        <li><a data-prefetch="true" data-transition="flip"
      href="app/views/transactions.html">Transactions</a></li>
        </ul>
      </div>
    </div>

    <script src="lib/require/require.js"
            data-main="app/main.js"></script>
</body>
</html>
```

As you can see, it is really similar to the standard "basic single page template" from the documentation (`http://demos.jquerymobile.com/1.4.4/pages/`), with the prefetching of the pages.

We load the style sheet of jQuery Mobile and our additional style sheet `styles.css`.

We put a fixed header and a fixed footer, with three links to the list page for each entity.

Then we tell RequireJS to load `main.js`,. which is in `app`.

We removed the script to load `cordova.js`, because we will load it with RequireJS too.

Now we create the main application file `main.js` under `app` with this code (a bit long, so I've split it with comments):

```
requirejs.config({
    baseUrl: "app/",
    paths: {
        "cordova": "../cordova",
        "jquery": "../lib/jquery/jquery-1.11.1.min",
    "jquery-mobile": "../lib/jquery-mobile/jquery.mobile-1.4.4.min",
        "knockout": "../lib/knockout/knockout-3.2.0"
    }
});
define(function (require) {
    var $ = require("jquery"),
        ko = require("knockout");
```

This is the standard starting code for any main module with RequireJS.

The application inside the device will execute from the /, so everything will work if you put /app as `baseUrl`.

When you develop with the `browser` plugin you should change the `baseUrl` to the folder of the computer you are using for the development.

For Windows users, if your code is inside `c:\KO\Ch4` you should use:

```
baseUrl: "/KO/Ch4/platforms/browser/www/app/"
```

For Linux/Mac users, if your code is inside /opt/ch4 you should use:

```
baseUrl: "/opt/ch4/platforms/browser/www/app/"
```

You can fix the problem in another way; use the following code for the `requirejs.config` function:

```
requirejs.config({
    baseUrl: "app/",
    paths: {
        "cordova": "../cordova",
        "jquery": "../lib/jquery/jquery-1.11.1.min",
        "jquery-mobile":
        "../lib/jquery-mobile/jquery.mobile-1.4.4.min",
        "knockout": "../lib/knockout/knockout-3.2.0",
        "services": "..//../services",
        "binding-handlers": "..//../binding-handlers"
    }
});
```

In this way, we keep `app/` as the `baseUrl`, and RequireJS can find the services and the binding-handlers using the right path.

```
var dd = $.Deferred(), jqmd = $.Deferred();
$(document).bind("mobileinit", jqmd.resolve);
document.addEventListener("deviceready", dd.resolve, false);
$.when(dd, jqmd).done(function() {
```

We want to be sure that jQuery Mobile and Cordova have loaded before we redirect to the first page because inside that page we will use Cordova plugins and functionalities of jQuery Mobile.

We wait for jQuery Mobile initialization using a deferred object ($(document).
bind("mobileinit", jqmd.resolve);), and another deferred object for Cordova
loading (document.addEventListener("deviceready", dd.resolve, false););
the resolution of both deferred will trigger the following application initialization code:

```
var pc = $.mobile.pageContainer;
pc.on("pagecontainerload", function (event, ui) {
  var url = ui.dataUrl.replace("views", "viewmodels")
                      .replace(".html", ".js");
  require([url], function (vm) {
    ko.applyBindings(new vm(), ui.page.get(0));
  });
});

var startingUrl = "accounts";
pc.pagecontainer("change",
                 "app/views/" + startingUrl + ".html",
                 {transition: "none"});

$("[data-role='navbar']").navbar();
$("[data-role='header'], [data-role='footer']").toolbar();
});
```

Here we perform three actions:

1. Register a callback on page change events.
2. Navigate from the current page (index) to the first view (Account List) we
   want to show.
3. Enhance the components (header, footer) we have inside the index page.

Any time the page changes, we get the new URL; take the View Model related to the
current View (we use the same convention we have seen with DurandalJS) and apply
it to the new View:

```
    require(["cordova", "jquery-mobile"]);
});
```

Then we use RequireJS to load both Cordova and jQuery Mobile asynchronously.

Now if we run the application we should have this:

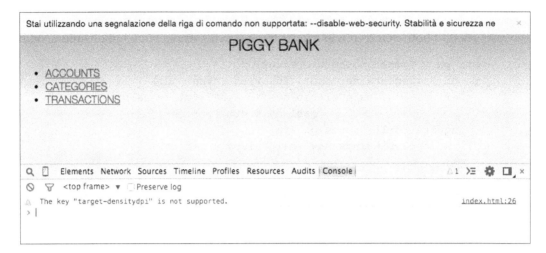

This is the ugly page we get before jQuery Mobile applies any modification; then we get this:

Here we get the starting page, with an **Error loading page** error, because it cannot find www/app/views/account.html

Finally, after a few seconds, the error message disappears:

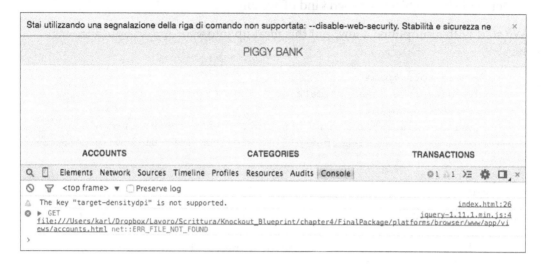

Let's fix this problem by creating the Account Module.

Making the list view with all the Accounts

Let's look at what the Account List page should look like:

In this View, we overwrite the header with a personalized one, keep the common footer, and show a block for each kind of account type.

We start with a simplified View; put this markup into `www/app/views/accounts.html`:

```
<div data-role="page">
  <div data-role="header" data-position="fixed">
    <h1>Accounts</h1>
    <button class="ui-btn ui-btn-right ui-btn-inline ui-mini
                   ui-corner-all ui-btn-icon-left ui-icon-plus">
      Add
    </button>
  </div>
```

The View is built around a div `page`, with a first block for the `header` (fixed in top).

Here we have the title of the page (inside the `h1` tag) and a button on the right to add accounts:

```
<div role="main" class="ui-content">
  <ul data-role="listview" data-split-icon="gear"
      data-inset="true" data-divider-theme="a">
    <li data-role="list-divider"></li>
    <li><a href="#"></a><a>Edit</a></li>
  </ul>
</div>
</div>
```

Then we have all the content inside the `main` block.

Here we put a `listview` for each account group, with a first line with the title of the group and a row for each account, with a link for the `show` functionality and an icon for the `edit` functionality.

Now you can launch the application again and you should get a working page
(but with errors):

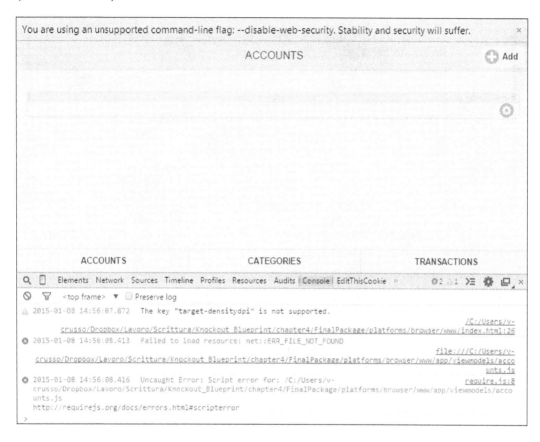

> If you get a broken page, it's because you probably have a problem
> with the baseUrl; recheck what I suggested before, and fix it.

Now we write the code of the tests (using a **Test-First Programming** process) and then we write the View Model; finally we add the binding inside the View.

Here, we are not using Test-Driven Development, just Test-First Programming.

Both terms refer to a programming process where you start writing the tests before the production code; if you are interested in TDD you can find many great books about the argument.

TFP is named in this way because we are going to write the specification of our View Model before the View Model itself; it is different from TDD because here we will write all the tests before any View Model code, to use them as specification of the product we are building.

If you look at the View, you can find all these features:

- `Get All`: This feature loads the list of all the accounts, showing a message to the user
- `Add`: This feature navigates to the Account Detail page
- `Edit`: This feature navigates to the Account Detail page for the selected item
- `Show`: This feature navigates to the Transaction List page

It should be a really bad design decision to put the code for the data loading inside a View Model, so we will use a `AccountDAO` module to manage the request to the data, and a `helper` module for the navigation code.

We received these with the Starting Package (inside `www/app/services`):

- `AccountDAO.js`: This exposes the functions to get, add, update, and delete any account
- `Helper.js`: This exposes the `navigateTo` function, a `getField` function to check whether a parameter is inside the query string, and also the `showMessage` and `hideMessage` helper functions

Putting the tests inside the bundle

For this chapter, we are going to use the development framework named Jasmine for testing (http://jasmine.github.io/2.0/introduction.html).

 There are many different frameworks you can use for testing, and you should try them all to find the best suited to your needs.

A (not exhaustive) list contains: QUnit, JSTestDriver, Jasmine, and Mocha.

Download the standalone bundle for Jasmine (Version 2.1.3 at the moment) from the website, and you'll get jasmine-standalone-2.1.3.zip.

Create the folder test under www and decompress the ZIP file inside this folder.

We can safely remove all the content of spec and the whole src folder.

Then we have to update SpecRunner.html at www/test to use RequireJS; replace the source files and the spec inclusion tags in this way:

```html
<script src="lib/jasmine-2.1.3/boot.js"></script>

<script src="../lib/require/require.js"></script>
<script>
  requirejs.config({
    baseUrl: "../app/",
    paths: {
      "jquery": "../lib/jquery/jquery-1.11.1.min",
      "jquery-mobile":
                  "../lib/jquery-mobile/jquery.mobile-1.4.4.min",
      "knockout": "../lib/knockout/knockout-3.2.0"
  }
  });  </script>

<!-- include source files here... -->

<!-- include spec files here... -->
<script src="spec/accounts.spec.js"></script>


</head>
```

When you work with Jasmine in this basic way, you put the specification inside the spec folder and update the `SpecRunner.html` adding all the specifications you want to test.

> You can see this way to work is not the best one, because you have to open a web page to look at the results of the tests; in a real-world scenario you should use a test-runner watching the tests/productions folder, to check continuously the state of the system.
>
> A really good system (I used it in many working places) is the usage of Grunt (`http://gruntjs.com`); it has many plugins to watch test folders, execute tests, and so on.

Now we can write the specifications in `www/test/spec/accounts.spec.js`:

```
describe("Accounts", function() {
  var $, viewModel, dao, helper;

  it("should load the AMD module", function(done) {
    require(["jquery", "viewmodels/accounts",
            "services/accountDAO", "services/helper"],
      function (_$, _viewModel, _dao, _helper) {
        $ = _$;
        viewModel = _viewModel;
        dao = _dao;
        helper = _helper;

        expect(viewModel).toBeDefined();

        done();
      });
  });
});
```

Here we are loading the required modules with the help of asynchronous test execution.

Our first test tries to load jQuery, and also the three modules we are going to use here; the main module is `viewModel`.

Testing with RequireJS can be tricky because you have to be sure you mock up all the unneeded dependencies before you use the module itself.

One of the best qualities of MVVM is the testability, so I suggest you learn how to develop a good test, what is TDD and BDD, and all other information about tests.

Here we load the `accountDAO` module and the `helper` module to mock them for our tests.

Any time you require a module, RequireJS caches the result; for this reason, each time you load the `AccountDAO` module you get an instance of the `AccountDAO` class (using the Singleton Design Pattern).

We are loading it here to be sure we mock the single instance; we will mock it later.

The last step we perform is to check whether `viewModel` is different than `null`, because we are going to instantiate it in the next tests.

If we were developing with TDD, we should now create the starting module for `www/app/viewmodels/accounts.js` with this code to make this first test work:

```
define(function(require) {
    return {};
});
```

Now we add more tests, just after the first function `it`:

```
describe("List", function() {

    beforeEach(function() {
        spyOn(dao, "getAll").and.callFake(function() {
            return $.when([]);
        });

        spyOn(helper, "navigateTo").and.callFake(function(url) {
            this.url = url;
        }.bind(this));

        this.vm = new viewModel();
    });
```

Before each real test, we ensure we have a new instance of the View Model we are testing and we mock the loading of the data from `AccountDAO` and the navigation.

Now we can start with all the test functions:

```
it("should populate property 'items'", function() {
  var items = this.vm.items();

  for (var i = 0; i < items.length; i++)
    expect(items[i].data().length).toEqual(0);
});
```

The first test is to be sure we have an array property named items, with an element for each kind of account (*cash, bank,* and so on) without any item inside:

```
it("should navigate to 'account' on add", function() {
  this.vm.add();

  expect(helper.navigateTo).toHaveBeenCalled();
  expect(this.url).toContain("account.html");
  expect(this.url).toContain("action=add");
});
```

Here we execute the add function, and we expect that the application will navigate to the account.html page with a parameter for the action to execute.

The next two tests are really similar to the last one, because when you edit an item or you visit one you should be redirected to other pages:

```
it("should navigate to 'account' on edit", function() {
  this.vm.edit({id: 1});

  expect(helper.navigateTo).toHaveBeenCalled();
  expect(this.url).toContain("account.html");
  expect(this.url).toContain("action=edit");
  expect(this.url).toContain("id=1");
});

it("should navigate to 'transactions' on show", function() {
  this.vm.show({id: 1});

  expect(helper.navigateTo).toHaveBeenCalled();
  expect(this.url).toContain("transactions.html");
  expect(this.url).toContain("source=account");
  expect(this.url).toContain("id=1");
});
});
```

Now it's time to check our specification; inside a browser, open `www/test/`
`SpecRunner.html`:

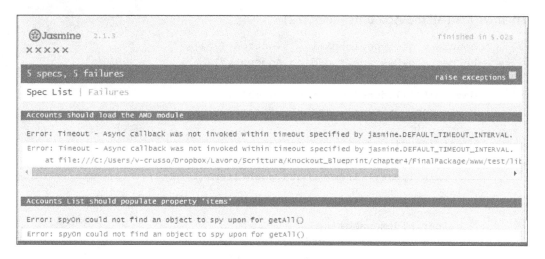

Now we can write the production code to fulfill all the tests, so edit the `accounts.js`
file under `www/app/viewmodels/` into this:

```
define(function (require) {
  var ko = require("knockout"),
      helper = require("services/helper"),
      dao = require("services/accountDAO");

  function Accounts() {
    this.items = ko.observableArray([
      { type: "cash", data: ko.observableArray([]),
        title: "Cash"},
      { type: "bank", data: ko.observableArray([]),
        title: "Bank account"},
      { type: "ccard", data: ko.observableArray([]),
        title: "Credit Card"}
    ]);

    this.loadAll();
  }
```

We are adding an observable array name `items` to this View Model, to keep all the
account types.

For each account type, we want to know the `title` to show in the View, the `type` to load the Accounts into the right array, and the list of items.

Then we load all the Accounts (`loadAll`):

```
Accounts.prototype.loadAll = function () {
  helper.showMessage("Loading Accounts");

  dao.getAll().done(function (items) {
    var map = ["cash", "bank", "ccard"];

    for (var i = 0; i < items.length; i++) {
      var index = map.indexOf(items[i].type);
      this.items()[index].data.push(items[i]);
    }

    helper.hideMessage();
  }.bind(this)).fail(function () {
    helper.showMessage("Something went wrong... ");
  });
};
```

The `loadAll` function uses the DAO function to get all the Accounts, and then it puts each loaded Account DAO into the data arrays.

Here we used the promises because the loading from the DAO is asynchronous (and is using promises internally); we also need to use the `.bind(this)` because inside the promise function we change the context (so `this` is not referring to the Account anymore):

```
Accounts.prototype.add = function () {
  helper.navigateTo("account.html?action=add");
};

Accounts.prototype.edit = function (account) {
  helper.navigateTo("account.html?action=edit" +
                                "&id=" + account.id);
};

Accounts.prototype.show = function (account) {
  helper.navigateTo("transactions.html?source=account" +
                                "&id=" + account.id);
};

  return Accounts;
});
```

These three functions simply navigate to the right page with additional parameters. If you look again, the tests we wrote previously use the right parameters. You can launch the `SpecRunner.html` test (under `www/test`) again and you'll get all tests passing:

Now that we have written the View Model and the tests, we can update the View with data binding; change `accounts.html` (under `www/app/views`) in this way (here I have skipped all the attributes except `data-bind`; do not remove them!):

```
<div>
  <div>
    <h1>Accounts</h1>
    <button data-bind="click: add">Add</button>
  </div>
  <div data-bind="foreach: items">
    <!-- ko if: data().length -->
    <ul>
      <li data-bind="text: title"></li>
      <!-- ko foreach: data -->
      <li>
        <a data-bind="click: $root.show.bind($root, $data),
                      text: name"></a>
        <a data-bind="click: $root.edit.bind($root, $data)">
          Edit <span data-bind="text: name"></span>
        </a>
      </li>
      <!-- /ko -->
    </ul>
    <!-- /ko -->
  </div>
</div>
```

Let's review all the changes.

Here we use a `listview` for each account group (`foreach: items`), but do not leave it empty (`if: data().length`), with the first line as the title of the group (`text: title`) and a row for each account (`foreach: data`) with a link for the `show` functionality and an icon for the `edit` functionality.

Now you can launch the application again and you should get a working page:

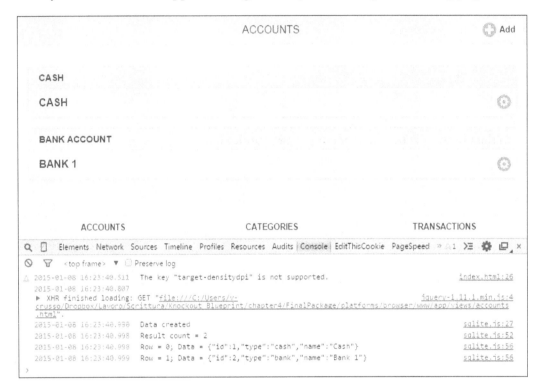

Adding the Detail page view

The Account List page was really easy to build, because it doesn't have much logic inside.

Here in the Account Detail page we will manage a single account, so we have to show all the information for a single account, and create/update one item.

Here, there is the wireframe of the Account Detail page:

The Account Detail page is shared between the functionalities `add` and `edit`.

Here, there are the differences inside the Views for the two functionalities:

Page type	Add Detail page	Edit Detail page
Title	New account	Update account
Button in the header	Create	Save
Fields	Empty	Filled with data
Button remove	No	After the fields

For the realization of this module we will follow a code-first approach, to show you both the ways you can test web applications.

We start with the View, because it's really simple; put this markup inside the `account.html` file under `www/app/views`:

```
<div data-role="page">
  <div data-role="header" data-position="fixed">
    <a href="#" data-rel="back"
       class="ui-btn ui-btn-left ui-alt-icon ui-nodisc-icon
       ui-corner-all ui-btn-icon-notext ui-icon-carat-l">Back</a>
    <!-- ko if: isNew -->
      <h1>New account</h1>
      <button class="ui-btn-right ui-btn ui-btn-inline ui-mini
                     ui-corner-all ui-btn-icon-left ui-icon-check"
```

```
                    data-bind="click: create, enable: canCreate">
          Create
        </button>
     <!-- /ko -->
     <!-- ko ifnot: isNew -->
       <h1>Update account</h1>
       <button class="ui-btn-right ui-btn ui-btn-inline ui-mini
                    ui-corner-all ui-btn-icon-left ui-icon-check"
            data-bind="click: save, enable: canSave">
          Save
        </button>
     <!-- /ko -->
  </div>
```

Actually we are showing a different header depending on the functionality: add or edit.

 Here we used the `<!-- ko if: isNew -->` notation; this kind of notation is useful when you can't use a container; you can find more information looking at the documentation for *Supporting virtual elements* at: `http://knockoutjs.com/documentation/custom-bindings-for-virtual-elements.html`

The problem with this code is the duplication of almost all the blocks; here, there is another implementation of this part:

```
<div data-role="header" data-position="fixed">
  <a href="#" data-rel="back" class="…">Back</a>
  <h1>
    <!-- ko if: isNew -->New<!-- /ko -->
    <!-- ko ifnot: isNew -->Update<!-- /ko -->
    account
  </h1>
  <button class="…" data-bind="click: act, enable: canAct">
    <!-- ko if: isNew -->Create<!-- /ko -->
    <!-- ko ifnot: isNew -->Save<!-- /ko -->
  </button>
</div>
```

As you can see here, we have less tag to manage, and the code is not harder than before to read.

This time the best implementation is the second one; we avoid duplicating tags, because all the options (isNew, !isNew) contain the same tag with different text.

You should go with the first implementation when you have different markup for different cases; so, for example this is bad practice:

```
<div data-role="header" data-position="fixed">
  <a href="#" data-rel="back" class="…">Back</a>
  <h1>
    <!-- ko if: isNew -->New<!-- /ko -->
    account
  </h1>
  <button class="…" data-bind="click: act, enable: canAct">
    <!-- ko ifnot: isNew -->Save<!-- /ko -->
  </button>
</div>
```

It's bad practice because here you need to look at all the markup to understand which tag will be shown depending on the state of the property isNew.

Now we can continue with our View:

```
<div role="main" class="ui-content">
  <label for="account-type" class="select">Type</label>
  <select data-bind="options: typesOfAccount,
                     value: type" id="account-type"></select>

  <label for="account-name">Name</label>
  <input type="text" id="account-name" data-bind="value: name">

  <!-- ko ifnot: isNew -->
  <button class="ui-shadow ui-btn ui-corner-all"
          data-bind="click: remove">Remove</button>
  <!-- /ko -->
  </div>
</div>
```

The main content shows a select list with all the possible types of Account (options: typesOfAccount), and a field for the account name (value: name).

Then, only if we are editing an existing item, we show the button to remove the item.

The View Model for this View should expose: isNew, act, canAct, typesOfAccount, type, name, and remove.

As you can see, it's a really simple View Model; let's put the following code into www/app/viewmodels/account.js:

```
define(function (require) {
  var ko = require("knockout"),
      helper = require("services/helper"),
      dao = require("services/accountDAO");

  function Account() {
    this.id = ko.observable();
    this.name = ko.observable();
    this.type = ko.observable();

    this.isNew = (helper.getField("action") === "add");

    this.canAct = ko.computed(function () {
      return (this.name() && this.type()) && true || false;
    }, this);

    if (!this.isNew) {
      this.load(helper.getField("id"));
    }
  }
}
```

After the modules have loaded, we define the View Model.

We expose the properties (id, name, and type) we want to show inside the fields and track whether we are adding a new item or editing an existing one (isNew); we use the mandatory properties to enable/disable the following action (canAct); and finally, if we are editing an existing item (!isNew), we ask the DAO to give us the item (load):

```
Account.prototype.load = function (id) {
  helper.showMessage("Loading Account");

  dao.getById(id).done(function (account) {
    this.id(account[0].id);
    this.name(account[0].name);
    this.type(account[0].type);

    helper.hideMessage();
  }.bind(this)).fail(function (err) {
    helper.showMessage("Something went wrong... " + err);
  });
};
```

The logic behind the loading is really simple, we ask the DAO to give us the item, and we use a promise to manage what happens later:

```
Account.prototype.act = function() {
  if (this.isNew) {
    this.create();
  } else {
    this.save();
  }
};
```

We updated the View to use the act function, so we have to redirect the execution to the right handler:

```
Account.prototype.create = function () {
  dao.create(this.name(), this.type()).done(function () {
    helper.showMessage("Account created");
    helper.navigateTo("accounts.html");
  }).fail(function (err) {
    helper.showMessage("Something went wrong... " + err);
  });
};

Account.prototype.save = function () {
  dao.updateById(this.name(), this.type(), this.id()
  ).done(function () {
    helper.showMessage("Account updated");
    helper.navigateTo("accounts.html");
  }).fail(function (err) {
    helper.showMessage("Something went wrong... " + err);
  });
};
```

The logic behind the creation and the saving is almost the same: we ask the DAO to perform the action, and then we show a message to the user and go back to the Accounts List page.

The last action we have is the removal of an existing item:

```
Account.prototype.remove = function () {
  //You should open a modal to ask to the user confirmation
  dao.removeById(this.id()).done(function () {
    helper.showMessage("Account removed");
```

```
      helper.navigateTo("accounts.html");
    }).fail(function (err) {
      helper.showMessage("Something went wrong... " + err);
    });
  };

  Account.prototype.typesOfAccount = ["cash","bank","ccard"];

  return Account;
});
```

We add the `typesOfAccount` property to the Account prototype because it's a shared property.

Before going to the tests, you should try the application, to see whether everything is working as expected:

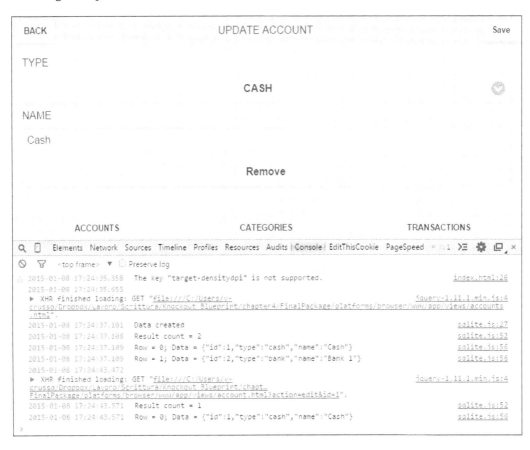

Enhancing the application with the unit tests

Now it's time to work on the test for this View Model.

First of all we have to update the `SpecRunner.html` file under `www/test` by adding a row with the new specification, just after the previous one:

```
<script src="spec/account.spec.js"></script>
```

Then, create the new spec `account.spec.js` under `www/test/spec`, and add the code to test all the features we already wrote:

```
describe("Account", function() {
  var $, viewModel, dao, helper;

  it("should load the AMD module", function(done) {
    require(["jquery", "viewmodels/account",
             "services/accountDAO", "services/helper"],
      function (_$, _viewModel, _dao, _helper) {
        $ = _$;
        viewModel = _viewModel;
        dao = _dao;
        helper = _helper;

        expect(viewModel).toBeDefined();

        done();
    });
  });
});
```

Here is the same logic we put in the previous starting test, checking for the dependencies.

Then we add the following tests after the previous function `it`:

```
describe("Form Add", function() {

  beforeEach(function() {
    spyOn(helper, "getField").and.callFake(function(param) {
      return "add";
    });

    spyOn(helper, "navigateTo").and.callFake(function(url){
      this.url = url;
```

```
    }.bind(this));

    this.vm = new viewModel();
  });
```

We modify the behavior of the functions `helper.getField` and `helper.navigateTo` (using the `spyOn` function of Jasmine), to ensure we pass the parameter `add` to the page, and to know which URL the application is navigating to:

```
it("should have empty properties on load", function() {
  expect(this.vm.id()).toBeUndefined();
  expect(this.vm.name()).toBeUndefined();
  expect(this.vm.type()).toBeUndefined();
});
```

We test the initial state of the properties; they should be `undefined`:

```
it("should disable creation on load", function() {
  expect(this.vm.canAct()).toEqual(false);
});

it("should disable creation with empty name", function() {
  this.vm.type("cash");

  expect(this.vm.canAct()).toEqual(false);
});

it("should enable creation otherwise", function() {
  this.vm.name("username");
  this.vm.type("cash");

  expect(this.vm.canAct()).toEqual(true);
});
```

We also check all the conditions where the user cannot add the item, and when all the mandatory properties are filled.

Here, I'm writing the code for the case `empty name`; for the other properties I leave the challenge to you to also write a test to make sure those are not empty:

```
it("should go to 'accounts' on creation", function() {
  spyOn(dao, "create").and.callFake(function() {
    return $.when(true);
  });
  this.vm.name("username");
```

```
        this.vm.type("cash");

        this.vm.create();

        expect(dao.create).toHaveBeenCalled();
        expect(helper.navigateTo).toHaveBeenCalled();
        expect(this.url).toContain("accounts.html");
    });
});
```

The last test checks what happens when you put the data and then add the Account.

We mock the call to the DAO, and then we check that it calls the `create` function and then redirects to the Accounts List page.

I leave to you, as an exercise, testing the code for this page when we are in editing mode.

Refactoring and working on the missing parts

The code for the Account CRUD is done and working, right? Or maybe there is something not working perfectly, caused from jQuery Mobile Widget enhancement?

Fixing KnockoutJS binding handler inside jQuery Mobile

If you create an Account with the type `bank`, and then you try to edit it, you'll see the `cash` type selected in the select field.

The reason behind this bug is that jQuery Mobile enhances the form components modifying the DOM structure, so you have to fix how the KnockoutJS binding handlers work in a few cases (like the `value`).

In this case, we have to modify the binding handler `value` to make it work with `select`; let's create `www/app/binding-handlers/selectValue.js`:

```
define(function (require) {
  var ko = require("knockout"),
      $ = require("jquery");

  ko.bindingHandlers.selectValue = {
```

```
        init: function (element, valueAccessor) {
          var value = valueAccessor(),
              $element = $(element);

          ko.bindingHandlers.value.init.apply(this, arguments);

          value.subscribe(function () {
            $element.selectmenu("refresh");
          });
        },
        update: ko.bindingHandlers.value.update
    };
});
```

With this binding handler, we apply the standard binding handler `value` for this element, then we subscribe to value changes, and we use the function `selectmenu.refresh` of jQuery Mobile to update the field text.

We have to update the View Model `account.js`, adding this row after the starting block of `require`, in this way:

```
        dao = require("services/accountDAO");
    require("binding-handlers/selectValue");

    function Account() {
```

We also have to update the `account.html` View by changing the `data-bind` attribute of the `select` from `value` to `selectValue`; we change this:

```
        <select data-bind="options: typesOfAccount,
                           value: type" id="account-type"></select>
```

In this way:

```
        <select data-bind="options: typesOfAccount,
                           selectValue: type"
        id="account-type"></select>
```

If you check the DOM enhanced from jQuery Mobile, you can see we have a `span` with the selected text drawn over the select field; we have to use the previous custom binding handler to update the text when we change the value of the bound property.

You can find similar problems with other code, such as the `enable` binding handler with the tag a.

When you use enhanced Widget with jQuery Mobile you should check whether everything is working properly.

For each kind of widget you use with a binding handler, you should check whether the DOM structure is different from what you expect, and use this as a hint to know where you should perform more fruition test.

Adding the contact plugin

Before going on, you should complete the missing Views or View Models:

- Transaction
- Transactions
- Category
- Categories

You can find the code for all of them inside the `additional_code` folder under www/ app/views and `additional_code` under www/app/viewmodels; move them into the parent folder.

As the next step, you should add the `Contacts` plugin to your project; go to the `PiggyBank` folder inside a shell and execute the following command:

`cordova plugin add org.apache.cordova.contacts`

Now we can use the plugin from our application.

If you try to access the contact list inside the browser you will get the error **Missing command error**, so, sorry but you cannot test this feature using the Browser plugin.

We add a button inside the `transaction.html` View, just after the text field for the customer, with this code:

```
<button type="button" data-bind="click: getContact">
    Get Contact from Device</button>
```

Then we add the function inside the `transaction.js` View Model; add the following code inside the module:

```
Transaction.prototype.getContact = function() {
    navigator.contacts.pickContact(function(contact){
        this.customer(contact.displayName ||
                    contact.name.formatted ||
        (contact.name.givenName + " " + contact.name.familyName));
    }.bind(this), function(err) {
        helper.showMessage(
            'Cannot select a contact: ' + err, 2000);
    });
};
```

If the Contact Picker gives us a contact, you take the information about the name; iOS doesn't support the `displayName` well; for this reason, we added the two other ways to get the name.

Now you should try this feature with a mobile device, because there is no way to check within your desktop browser.

 The only way you can test the application is with your mobile device after you build the application.

As you can see, it's really easy to add features with the help of the plugins.

You can find many other plugins at: `http://docs.phonegap.com/en/3.5.0/cordova_plugins_pluginapis.md.html`

Publishing the application

We are not going to see how to publish the application, but you can follow the guide at: `https://build.phonegap.com/`

Summary

In this chapter, we built a full hybrid mobile application.

We used jQuery Mobile for the internal structure, Cordova to get the additional features of the device (such as the contacts), and KnockoutJS to bind them all.

Most of all, we have seen how to test a KnockoutJS application with code-first and test-first techniques.

Now that you know how to apply tests to MVVM applications, you should do it in each web application you make.

In the next chapter, we will see another SPA built with DurandalJS, how to manage a wizard, and what we should do for the SEO.

5
Wizard for the Public Administration

We already have seen how to build an SPA with DurandalJS, in *Chapter 3*, *SPA for Timesheet Management*.

In this chapter, we are going to build another SPA, but this time the main goals of the chapter will be accessibility and SEO.

This is the list of topics we will cover in this chapter:

- How to realize a multipage wizard with the help of DurandalJS
- **Graceful degradation**, **Progressive Enhancement**, and what's best for an SPA.
- Which kind of accessibility rules can we follow if we plan an SPA?
- Best practice to do a good SEO when you have a highly dynamic web application.
- How to realize a fully accessible, search-engine-optimized, and responsive Single Page Application.

We will see all the best practices re-creating a deployed real-world application used in Italy to simplify all the paperwork needed to relocate.

The project, a real-world web application

This project will follow the steps to create the web application you can find at: http://www.caprapido.it/en (actual redirection of http://www.caprapido.com).

When you want to relocate, in Italy, you have to:

1. Fill a really long paper module.
2. Take it to the public office of the new municipality you want to relocate to.
3. Wait for a public officer to come to your house to check whether you really live there.
4. And then, if you don't get any notification before the 45th day, it's done.

We cannot do anything for the third and fourth step, but we can help people with the first two.

The web application you can find online contains three different modules:

- **Relocate**: This module helps people with the paperwork for the public administration
- **Manage addresses**: This module is a single point to check who knows your address, and to manage auto-updating after a change
- **Company access**: This module is a portal for the companies, to use the service

In this chapter, we are going to see how to develop the web application for the Relocate module, because it was realized respecting the best practices for accessibility and SEO with KnockoutJS.

The reason behind the three modules I wrote before was:

- The Relocate module is to acquire new users
- The Manage addresses module is to keep them engaged
- The Company access module is where we get paid

So, after the user knows the web application, he can use it to share and change the address information given to the companies; and the company should pay us for our always updated information.

For this reason, we need to get a really good ranking inside the search engines.

In fact, this module was realized respecting all the following requirements:

- Fully accessible (WCAG 2.0)
- Easy to use
- Realized with SEO in mind, to have a good ranking
- Fluid layout (responsive)

Looking at the big picture of the project

Let's start checking how the wireframe of the whole web application should be when you land on it:

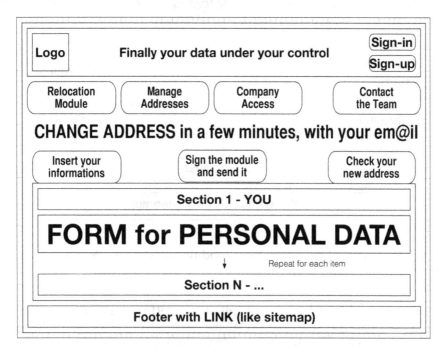

You can see that the Relocation module is built at the center of the page, after the section with the logo and the navigation links and before the footer with the links.

To be focused on the topics listed at the beginning, we are not going to build the web application from scratch; it would be really too extensive for a single chapter, and we would talk about out-of-topic arguments too much.

So, instead of downloading all the libraries (DurandalJS, KnockoutJS, RequireJS, and so on) as you have done in *Chapter 3, SPA for Timesheet Management*, let's download the StartingPackage.zip file from the Packt Publishing website, unzipping its content into a new folder for the project, named CAPrapido.

Reviewing the content we got for free

Inside the package, you can find a full starting SPA performed with DurandalJS.

You can easily check that the `shell` module (`CAPrapido/app/views/shell.html`) contains the markup to render the following wireframe:

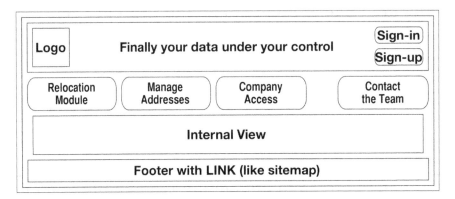

If you check the source code of the `shell` module you can see it's full of the `role` and `aria` attributes and semantic tags.

Accessible Rich Internet Applications (**ARIA**) is a set of accessibility attributes used to make HTML more accessible; you use them adding `aria` and `role` attributes inside the markup.

There is more to discuss about accessibility, but so as to not become boring, we now start with the Relocate module, and we will discuss and add all the accessibility code later.

Analysing and developing the Relocate module

With this module, we want to transpose the module for the relocation from the paper form into a digital web form.

We have already seen the steps the user has to follow to perform relocation; we will define three steps to help him with the full workflow:

1. Fill the form.

2. Sign and send.

3. Wait 45 days and then manage your address.

Here there is a wireframe of these steps:

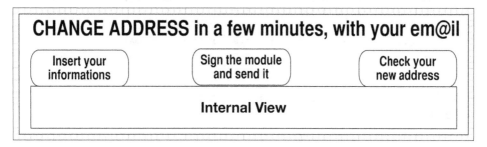

Realizing such a kind of interface is really simple with DurandalJS, with the help of the child router.

The `router` binding handler gives us a way to modularize the contents of the Views, separating them from the layout of the container.

We can go further with this modularization, with the use of the child router; inside a module, we define the children routes we want to show and the router plugin will activate all the modules for the selected path.

You can find a good example of how the child router works inside the examples of DurandalJS, looking at the ko route.

Just remember that you have to set the `baseUrl` inside the `main.js` file to an absolute path to everything working with the `pushState` enabled.

The `relocate` module route points to `viewmodels/relocate/index`; we will put the logic for the module and the routing information for the inner modules here.

Let's start updating the View Model `viewmodels/relocate/index.js` putting this code:

```
define(["plugins/router", "knockout"], function (router, ko) {
    var childRouter = router.createChildRouter().makeRelative({
        moduleId: "viewmodels/relocate",
        fromParent: true
    }).map([
```

Here we create a new child router, and ask DurandalJS to consider all the routes we are going to define to start with `viewmodels/relocate.`:

```
{
    route: ["","fill-the-form"], moduleId: "fill-the-form",
    title: "Insert your information", nav: true,
    hash: "relocate/fill-the-form"
```

```
    }, {
      route: "sign-and-send", moduleId: "sign-and-send",
      title: "Sign the module and send it", nav: true
    }, {
      route: "wait-45-days", moduleId: "wait-45-days",
      title: "Check your new address", nav: true
    }
```

We now define the three routes; here you cannot find any difference with the routes from the main router:

```
    ]).buildNavigationModel();

  return {
    router: childRouter
  }
});
```

We expose the `childRouter` as `router`, as suggested in the documentation of DurandalJS (`http://durandaljs.com/documentation/Using-The-Router.html`).

Now we use the new `childRouter` function inside the View `views/relocate/index.html`:

```
<section class="container-fluid relocate">
  <header>
    <h2>CHANGE ADDRESS in a few minutes, with your email</h2>
    <ul class="nav nav-tabs" role="tablist"
        data-bind="foreach: router.navigationModel">
      <li role="presentation"
          data-bind="css: { active: isActive }">
        <a role="tab" data-toggle="tab"
           data-bind="attr: { href: hash }, text: title"></a>
      </li>
    </ul>
  </header>
```

Here, we are using the same code you can find in the header of the page for the navigation, nothing special:

```
<main class="page-host" id="content" role="main"
      data-bind="router: {
                   transition:'entrance',
                   cacheViews:true
                 }">
  </main>
</section>
```

Here, we are using the `router` binding again to show the internal Views.

As you can see, here we have code for the classes of Bootstrap (such as `container-fluid`), and roles, ARIA, and semantic tags (such as `header`, `main`).

I know that they make the markup harder to read, but they are here to help you to see how to make real code, not oversimplified one; I'll try to keep it simple when I can, but be prepared to see many classes for the styles.

If you try to load the application (the best way is using `http-server`), you should get a page like this one:

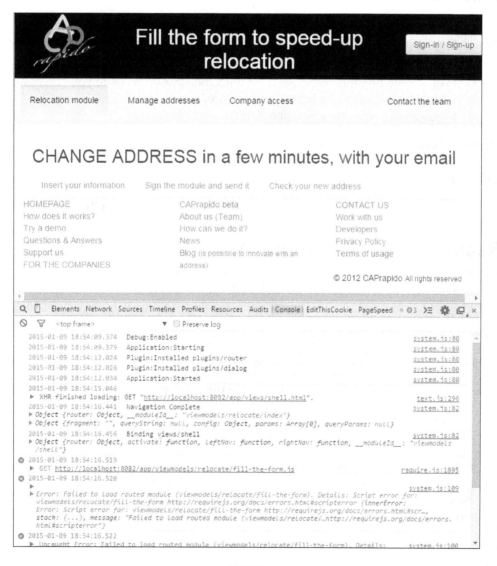

As you can see, we get an error because the fill-the-form module doesn't exist.

Before going to the code of this first module, let's quickly discuss which is the best way to realize this application.

Graceful Degradation versus Progressive Enhancement

When you start to realize a web application you have to choose which direction you want to follow:

- Graceful Degradation: Starting from the best website you can realize, and then applying all the patches you need to get an acceptable experience for the older browser

- Progressive Enhancement: Starting with the simpler website you can realize with all the mandatory paths covered, and then adding the CSS and the JavaScript as an enhancement for the modern browser

The main benefits of the Progressive Enhancement is that you can be sure all users will be able to fully use your website, it's easy to fulfill the accessibility requirements, and the page is best suited for SEO.

So, why should you realize a website differently if you can have all these benefits?

Reasoning against Progressive Enhancements

There are almost two good reasons why you can choose to avoid following the Progressive Enhancement path; let's look at them.

First of all, you can find one thought on this path from KnockoutJS's main contributor (Steven Sanderson) at the following URL:

`https://groups.google.com/d/msg/knockoutjs/UahPJPzMuUU/kJLaTDuL9EYJ`

Here is a brief quote of his intervention inside the thread:

> *To expand and clarify on Alisson's point, since KO is all about MVVM-in-the-browser, the scenario it targets always involves JavaScript.*

> *In this case, and particularly as your app behaviors get more sophisticated, this goes way beyond what's possible with progressive enhancement. In my experience, most people who want to build sophisticated behaviors quickly find that trying to structure the code in a progressive enhancement style becomes counter-productive.*

...

> *I'm not against progressive enhancement in principle; I just find it a very*
> *suboptimal pattern if you're requiring JavaScript anyway.*

Obviously, we shouldn't blindly trust what he says, but probably he knows
what he says about KnockoutJS and Progressive Enhancement, being the
creator of KnockoutJS.

The second reason against that path is relative to the framework we are going to
use: DurandalJS.

Applying KnockoutJS binding to an already built web application is not so hard or
problematic till you apply focus to single pages, but this time we are going to realize
an SPA with DurandalJS.

As you already saw in *Chapter 3, SPA for Timesheet Management*, DurandalJS uses an
internal client router to manage all the routes; it means that if you build a full static
page, when you apply JavaScript to enhance it, it will drop all the dynamic parts to
build them again with client data.

For this reason, you will build a nice application for people with JavaScript disabled,
but a really bad experience to all the other users, downloading more data than
needed, and getting a double-rendered page.

For those reasons, we are not going to follow the Progressive Enhancement path for
this project.

Making the form for the first child route

The first route will contain the form; the module is really long, so we will split it into
multiple sections (using an `Accordion` widget).

We also try to follow the guidelines you can find at: `https://html.spec.whatwg.`
`org/multipage/forms.html#forms`

Let's begin with the first section.

Asking for personal information

The first section asks the user for personal information; here is the extract of the module:

Last name *			Sex *
First name *		Date of birth *	
Place of Birth *		Marital status *	
Citizenship *		Tax Code *	
Position in the profession when employed: **			
☐ Entrepreneur / Freelancer	☐ Manager / Employee		☐ Worker on their own
☐ Workman and assimilated	☐ Assistant		
Non-professional status **			
☐ Housewife ☐ Student	☐ Unemployed / seeking first		☐ Retiree / retired from work
☐ Other non-professional			
Education school leaving certificate **			
☐ No certificate / elementary school certificate		☐ Secondary school certificate	
☐ High school certificate ☐ Bachelor's degree	☐ University degree		☐ Doctorate
Driving licence type ***			
Number ***			
Date of issue ***			
Issuing Office ***		Province of ***	
Vehicles number plates registered in Italy as owner/co- owner, usufructuary /lessee ***			
Motor vehicles ***			
Trailers ***			
Motorcycles ***			
Mopeds ***			

As you can see, the user has to fill many fields.

Let's define a convention about boilerplate code for the module.

Boilerplate for the module `Person` (inside the `relocate/fill-the-form` folder) means:

Create a folder `relocate/fill-the-form` inside both the `views` and `viewmodels` folders; then create the View Model `viewmodels/relocate/fill-the-form/person.js` with this content:

```
define(function(require) {
  function PersonViewModel() {
  };

  return PersonViewModel;
});
```

Finally put a View `views/relocate/fill-the-form/person.html` with this markup:

```
<section></section>
```

Create a boilerplate module for each route we defined: `fill-the-form`, `sign-and-send`, and `wait-45-days` inside the `relocate` folder.

Then update the View `fill-the-form.html` by adding:

```
<form class="form-horizontal" role="form">
  <section id="collapsePerson" class="not-a-section">
    <header class="section">
      <h3>SECTION 1 - I, THE UNDERSIGNED</h3>
    </header>
    <!-- ko
           compose: "viewmodels/relocate/fill-the-form/person"
    --> <!-- /ko -->
  </section>
</form>
```

Here we have a section with the header, and then we'll show you the `Person` module.

This is the real markup you find in the website; it uses the `accordion` widget to enhance the UX, but as you can see, the markup is dirtier and harder to understand than the previous one:

```
<form class="form-horizontal" role="form">
  <section class="panel-group" id="mainModule">
    <section class="panel panel-default">
      <header class="panel-heading row">
        <a class="panel-title" data-toggle="collapse"
           data-parent="#mainModule"
           href="#collapsePerson">
          <h3 class="col-sm-12">
            SECTION 1 - I, THE UNDERSIGNED
          </h3>
        </a>
      </header>
      <section id="collapsePerson"
               class="panel-collapse collapse"
               data-bind='compose:
          "viewmodels/relocate/fill-the-form/person"'>
      </section>
    </section>
  </section>
</form>
```

Then we define the `Person` module, which we just used, to manage all this data; so we create the boilerplate for this module (inside a new folder `relocate/fill-the-form`) that we already added to the `fill-the-form` View.

Now that we show the `Person` module, we should think about it, and how to render it in the easiest and simple-to-use way.

To get a better UX, we will apply three ideas to this form:

1. We use metaphors from the real world to render the visual appearance of the physical card.
2. We try to automate the filling of fields if possible (such as the `Tax Code`).
3. We transform select-based fields into a more visual one, with the help of images.

The first component for the `Person` we realize is the `Identity Card`; here we put all the fields for personal information.

We start creating the boilerplate for the new `identity-card` module (inside the `relocate/fill-the-form` folder) and then add it to the `Person` View.

Change `person.html` by adding this:

```
<section class="not-a-section">
  <!-- ko
  compose: "viewmodels/relocate/fill-the-form/identity-card"
    --> <!-- /ko -->
</section>
```

The idea here is that this will be a container for the whole person form, so we should add any other additional module (such as the `marital-status`, or the `driving-license` module) here. So now we start showing the first new component: `identity-card`.

Now we can build the `identity-card` module.

Here there is a wireframe of this component:

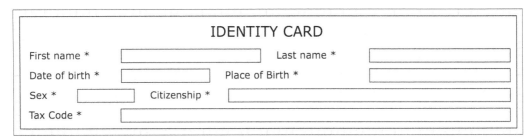

To give good accessibility to this module, we have to use the `label` tags, the `autocomplete` attribute, and `placeholder` in the right way.

Let's create `identity-card.html` following all these points:

```
<section class="section" id="identity-section">
  <header class="row">
    <h4 class="col-sm-12">IDENTITY CARD</h4>
  </header>
```

Here we have our headers with an `h4` tag, because the previous header was an `h3`:

> A rule about accessibility states that the heading tag should be used to explain the information hierarchy.

```
<fieldset>
  <div class="form-group">
    <label for="first-name" class="col-sm-2 control-label">
      First Name
    </label>
    <div class="col-sm-4">
      <input type="text" class="form-control" id="first-name"
             autocomplete="firstname" placeholder="John"
             data-bind="textInput: firstName">
    </div>
```

Inside a `fieldset`, we put all the labels with the relative fields.

As you can see, for our `firstname` field, we use a `label` with the `for` attribute pointing to the `input` field; for this reason, we need to add an `id` to the field.

> Pay attention when you use the `id` attribute, inside an SPA; the `id` attribute must be unique across all the applications, so try to avoid them if possible, or give them the `namespace` name.
>
> For example, here you should use `identity-first-name` or something similar.

We also use the `autocomplete` attribute, and a `placeholder`.

 As I pointed out before, writing real accessible code needs many more lines than we have seen in previous chapters; try to adhere to this kind of code every time you develop for the Internet.

To keep the code here clean, I'll skip all the attributes for the accessibility and the visual aspect; I'll keep only the classes for the column number (`col-sm-x` as you can see in the Bootstrap documentation); you can use this first example to add them by yourself.

The next field is really similar to this first one:

```
<label class="col-sm-2">Last Name</label>
<div class="col-sm-4">
  <input type="text" data-bind="textInput: lastName">
</div>
</div>
```

The next row will contain two different kinds of fields: a `dateinput` field and a `select` field:

```
<div class="form-group">
  <label class="col-sm-2">Date of birth</label>
  <div class="col-sm-3">
    <input type="date" data-bind="textInput: birthDate">
  </div>

  <label class="col-sm-3">Place of birth</label>
  <div class="col-sm-4">
    <select data-bind="options: communes,
                       optionsText: textForCommune,
                       value: birthPlace,
                  optionsCaption: 'Place of birth'"></select>
  </div>
</div>
```

Inside the View Model we will load, with a call to the server API, the list of communes (`communes`).

The next field is sex; we start adding it as a normal `select` field, then we will enhance to a nicer one using icons:

```
<div class="form-group">
  <label class="col-sm-1">Sex</label>
  <div class="col-sm-2">
    <select data-bind="options: typeOfSex,
                       value: sex,
                       optionsCaption:'Choose a sex'"></select>
  </div>
  <label class="col-sm-2">Citizenship</label>
  <div class="col-sm-7">
    <input type="text" data-bind="textInput: citizenship">
  </div>
</div>
```

The sex `select` field is really simple; we could put the markup for the values directly inside the form, but in this way we keep all the `select` fields inside the form uniform.

The last field we'll show you is a computed one, dependent on each other field here:

```
<div class="form-group">
  <label class="col-sm-2">Tax Code</label>
  <div class="col-sm-10">
    <p class="form-control-static"
       data-bind="text: taxCode"></p>
  </div>
</div>
    </fieldset>
  </section>
```

Look how many lines; I hid many classes, but nonetheless the number of lines is bigger than the code for our binding with KnockoutJS.

I'm remarking on this point because in the previous chapters every View was full of bindings; it's OK when you keep all the code simple, but in a real-life code, it is easier to find code such as this.

Let's write the View Model for the latest view, `identity-card.js`:

```
define(function (require) {
  var ko = require("knockout"),
    personHelper = require("services/personHelper"),
    communeRepository = require("services/communeRepository");
```

We require two modules, `personHelper` and `communeRepository`.

The first module contains helper methods such as `calculateTaxCode`; the second contains the `findAll` method to get access to the commune list:

```
function IdentityCardViewModel() {
  this.firstName = ko.observable();
  this.lastName = ko.observable();
  this.birthDate = ko.observable();
  this.birthPlace = ko.observable();
  this.sex = ko.observable();
  this.citizenship = ko.observable();

  this.taxCode = ko.pureComputed(function () {
    return personHelper.calculateTaxCode(
      this.firstName(), this.lastName(), this.sex(),
      this.birthDate() && new Date(this.birthDate()),
      this.birthPlace());
  }, this);
}
```

We are simply defining all the fields we used in the View; we are also defining the `taxCode` as a computable observable, depending on all the other fields.

> Here we use a `pureComputed` function instead of a normal one; this kind of computed can improve the performance, but we can use this only if the function it decorates has no side effects, as in this case.

```
IdentityCardViewModel.prototype.typeOfSex = ["Male", "Female"];

IdentityCardViewModel.prototype.communes = [];
communeRepository.findAll().then(function (data) {
  IdentityCardViewModel.prototype.communes = data;
});

IdentityCardViewModel.prototype.textForCommune = function(c) {
  return c.commune + " (" + c.province + ")";
};

    return IdentityCardViewModel;
});
```

Here we define the class-level properties, `typeOfSex` and `communes`.

At this point, without applying all the style, id, and classes that we should apply, the application should look like this:

Fixing a hidden bug

If you double-check this last code you can find a well-hidden bug.

There is a race condition inside the loading of the `communes`.

Probably during the development you'll never see this problem, because the time needed to load the JSON inside the repository is relatively smaller than the time needed to do the composition.

But if you try to use this code in a production environment, you'll see this kind of behavior:

The problem is that we are asynchronously loading the list of communes and are putting it inside a property; here we have a normal property, not an observable array, so KnockoutJS doesn't know that it should update the View.

The simpler solution is the wrapping of the property inside an `observableArray`, such as the following:

```
IdentityCardViewModel.prototype.communes = ko.observableArray([]);
communeRepository.findAll().then(function (data) {
  IdentityCardViewModel.prototype.communes(data);
});
```

While we are fixing it, we can also improve the behavior to give the user a better experience: let's show a `loading` text during the initialization and substitute it with the options after the loading.

Adding a new binding handler for the asynchronous loading

This kind of binding handler seems reusable in many contexts: with `options`, with `foreach`, with `template`, and so on.

For this reason, let's split it into two different binding handlers:

- `loading`
- `optionsLoading`

Let's use the folder named `app/binding-handlers` by adding a new file `loading.js` inside it with the following content:

```
define(function (require) {
  var ko = require("knockout"),
    $ = require("jquery"),
    composition = require("durandal/composition");

  ko.bindingHandlers["loading"] = {
```

We need KnockoutJS and jQuery, and this time we also get the `composition` object we need because this binding handler should be executed after the `compositionComplete` event:

```
init: function (element) {
  var $element = $(element),
      loading = $("<div>Loading... " +
        "<i class='fa fa-spinner fa-spin fa-2x'></i></div>"),
      position = $element.position(),
```

```
        $parent = $element.parent();

    loading.css({
      position: "absolute",
      left: position.left+2, top: position.top+2,
      width: $parent.width()-4, height: $parent.height()-4,
      "text-align": "center", background: "white"
    });

    $element.after(loading);
  },
```

We create a new `div` with the spinning icon, and put it after the current element; we modify the dimension of this `div`, to cover the components of the binding.

We cannot use a simple class here because we need to receive the position of the bound item:

```
    update: function (element, valueAccessor) {
      var value = ko.utils.peekObservable(valueAccessor()),
        $element = $(element);

      if (value.length === 0) {
        ko.utils.unwrapObservable(valueAccessor());
      } else {
        $element.next().remove();
      }
    }
  };
```

Here, we will create the logic for the `once` update: we keep the loading `div` over the current element while the `observableArray` is empty.

We used two KnockoutJS helper functions:

- `ko.utils.peekObservable`: This function gets the value inside the observable without notifying the observer
- `ko.utils.unwrapObservable`: This function gets the value inside the observable (if the property is an observable) or the value (if it's not an observable)

Now for the last lines of the module:

```
    composition.addBindingHandler("loading");
});
```

As the last step, we ensure this binding will be executed after the attaching of the View.

If you double-check this solution, you can find a flaw in a use case: if we get zero elements from the server during the update of the `observableArray`, we will never remove the `loading` text.

In our use case, this is not a problem, but if you find it a problem for you, you should put an additional solution, maybe with a timer to manage the timeout.

Now we create the binding handler `optionsLoading` (as `binding-handlers/optionsLoading.js`):

```
define(function (require) {
  var ko = require("knockout"),
      $ = require("jquery"),
      composition = require("durandal/composition");
  require("binding-handlers/loading");

  composition.addBindingHandler("optionsLoading", {
    init: function () {
      ko.bindingHandlers.loading.init.apply(this, arguments);
      ko.bindingHandlers.options.init.apply(this, arguments);
    },
```

We are reusing the `loading` binding handler we built previously, and then we execute the `options` binding handler:

```
    update: function (element, valueAccessor) {
      var value = ko.utils.peekObservable(valueAccessor()),
        $element = $(element);

      if (value.length === 0) {
        ko.utils.unwrapObservable(valueAccessor());
      } else {
        ko.bindingHandlers.options.update.apply(this, arguments);
        $element.next().remove();
      }
    }
  });
});
```

As you can see, the logic is almost the same of the previous code, but here we execute the `options.update` function to fill the `select` with the data.

The main reason I didn't reuse the previous code here is because I didn't want to add promises or callbacks into the `loading.update` function.

If you want to use it, consider that jQuery give us promises; just remember that the `update` function is executed more and more, but is defined just once.

Now we can update the View Model `identity-card.js` adding this `require` at the beginning of the file, after the other `require` calls:

```
require("binding-handlers/optionsLoading");
```

Update the View `identity-card.html` also, replacing the bind `options:communes` with the new `optionsLoading:communes` one; let's update:

```
<select data-bind="options: communes,
                   optionsText: textForCommune,
                   value: birthPlace,
                   optionsCaption: 'Place of birth'"></select>
```

With:

```
<select data-bind="optionsLoading: communes,
                   optionsText: textForCommune,
                   value: birthPlace,
                   optionsCaption: 'Place of birth'"></select>
```

Now the page should look like this:

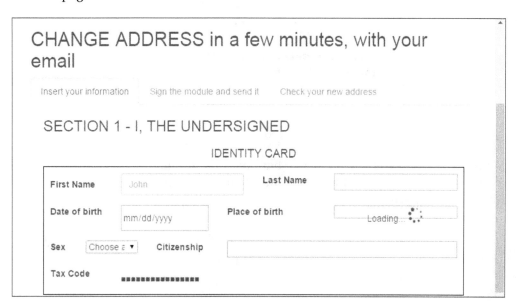

Now we can continue with the enhancement of the field for the selection of the sex.

Enhancing the selection fields

The selection field is a good standard way to show the gender selection; but here we want to give the user a better UX, so we change the `select` field with two images, visually describing the gender.

To do this, replace the following code inside `identity-card.html`:

```
<label class="col-sm-1>Sex</label>
<div class="col-sm-2">
  <select data-bind="options: typeOfSex, value: sex,
                optionsCaption: 'Choose a sex'"></select>
</div>
```

With this one:

```
<label class="col-sm-1 control-label">Gender</label>
<div class="col-sm-2">
  <!-- ko foreach: typeOfSex -->
  <div class="enhanced-radio col-sm-6"
      data-bind="css: {
            active: $parent.isActive($data, $parent.sex)
                }">
    <button type="button" class="sex text-center"
            data-bind="attr: {
                        'aria-label': label,
                        'data-value': label
                      },
        click: $parent.setActive.bind($data, $parent.sex)">
        <i class="fa fa-2x" data-bind="css: icon"></i>
      </button>
  </div>
  <!-- /ko -->
</div>
```

In this way, we are going to show two buttons with an icon inside; we add the `active` class for the selected item, and an action (`setActive`) to update the current selected item.

Now we have to update the View Model to reflect the changes we have made; update `identity-card.js` adding these lines:

```
IdentityCardViewModel.prototype.isActive = function(vm, p) {
    return p() === vm.value;
};

IdentityCardViewModel.prototype.setActive = function(p, d) {
    p(d.value);
};
```

With `isActive`, we check whether the value of the current item is the same as the value of the given property; with `setActive`, we update this value.

Then replace the definition of `typeOfSex` with the following code:

```
IdentityCardViewModel.prototype.typeOfSex = [
    { value: "male",   label: "Male",   icon: "fa-male"   },
    { value: "female", label: "Female", icon: "fa-female" }
];
```

The code for the rest of the form is similar to what we have seen till now, so I leave it to you to do it; so, let's see what we should do to make the code accessible.

Updating the code to be accessible

In this section, we are going to create a widget to substitute the code for the gender field.

Before going with the code, let's see what you should know about accessibility.

A few words about accessibility

Before starting with the code, I just wanted to point out to you some information about accessibility.

You can find the most important guidelines for accessibility at these URLs:

- `http://www.w3.org/TR/WCAG20/`
- `http://www.w3.org/WAI/PF/aria-practices/#accessiblewidget`

I found the easiest way to build an accessible web application is by following the hints found at the *Google I/O 2011* presentation:

- Use clean HTML and use standard tags whenever possible
- Manage focus
- Add key handlers
- Add ARIA for screen readers

Remember also to download and use additional software (such as the ones you can find at: `http://www.w3.org/WAI/ER/tools/`) to check the code you write for the accessibility.

These are some tools I suggest you use:

- `ChromeShades`, `Wave Toolbar`, and `HTML_CodeSniffer` are good tools to use during the development phase
- `ChromeVox` and mouse unplugging can be useful to test how the site appears to people with disabilities

Making the gender field accessible

We will start with one of the following examples from this URL: `http://test.cita.illinois.edu/aria/radio/index.php`

We are going to use the radio example because the `gender` field should be represented with a `select` or a `radio role`; we show all the items at once, so the `radio role` is the best solution.

Update the `identity-card.html` View removing the `label` and the `div` with the `enhanced-sex` id and put these rows:

```
<label for="gender" class="col-sm-1 control-label">Gender</label>

<ul class="col-sm-2" id="gender" tabindex="0" role="radiogroup"
    data-bind="radio-ally: sex">
  <!-- ko foreach: typeOfSex -->
  <li class="enhanced-radio col-sm-6" tabindex="-1" role="radio"
      aria-checked="false"
      data-bind="attr: {
                id: 'gender-' + value,
                'data-value': value
            }">
```

```
        <i class="fa fa-2x" role="presentation"
            data-bind="css: icon"></i>
        <span class="sr-only" data-bind="text: label"></span>
    </li>
    <!-- /ko -->
</ul>
```

Here we replace the container div with an ul, and apply the radio-a11y binding handler to it; then we changed the buttons with li tags, and we added id and data-value to be used inside the binding handler.

We show the icon all the time, and we hide the text (text: label) except for the screen reader (sr-only, a class from Bootstrap to be shown only using a screen reader).

I put the binding handler inside the Starting Package because it is really big; I updated it to use jQuery, so you should be able to read and understand it.

Then we have to load the new binding handler inside the identity-card.js View Model; add this row at the beginning of the file:

```
require("binding-handlers/radio-a11y");
```

We can also remove both the functions to manage the active class; we will use the binding handler to manage it; remove both the functions from the code:

```
IdentityCardViewModel.prototype.isActive = function(vm, p) {...};
IdentityCardViewModel.prototype.setActive = function(p, d) {...};
```

With this binding handler we now have a fully accessible ARIA-enabled radio-group widget.

Updating the loading binding handler for accessibility

The loading binding handler we developed a few paragraphs ago is working well but is not accessible.

Luckily, it's easy to make it accessible, we just need to add the right aria attributes.

We start updating the loading.js binding handler:

1. Add the role progressbar to the loading div:

    ```
    loading = $('<div aria-label="Ajax loading data" '+
                    'role="progressbar">Loading... '+
                '<i class="fa fa-spinner fa-spin fa-2x"'+
                    'aria-hidden="true"></i></div>'),
    ```

2. After the `$element.after(loading);` row, add the following code with the `aria` attributes:

```
$element.attr({
        "aria-busy": true,
        "aria-live": "polite",
        "aria-describedby": $element.get(0).id
    });
```

3. Update the `aria-busy` attribute of the element when we remove the `loading` div; after the `$element.next().remove();` line, append the following code:

```
$element.attr("aria-busy", false);
```

4. Execute the third step with the `optionsLoading` binding handler again.

And we are done.

In this way, we indicate that we are updating the field when we show the loading message with `aria-busy=true`; then, after the remote loading of the data, we use it again in `aria-busy=false` to give the screen reader the knowledge of the change.

Here we have seen two applications of accessibility to this project; we should do this for each custom component we realize.

Now that we have seen how to update the web application to be accessible, we can finally look at the last topic of this chapter — making the web application **SEO-crawlable**.

Working to make the app SEO crawlable

If you think that making an SPA crawlable should be hard to accomplish, it's time to change your mind.

If you look at the documentation of DurandalJS you can find how to make the application crawable (at least, from Google Search).

For this section, we are going to follow the guide at: `http://durandaljs.com/documentation/Making-Durandal-Apps-SEO-Crawlable.html`.

The first step should be the modification of our page to contain the `fragment` meta tag.

Add the following code inside the `head` tag of `index.html`:

```
<meta name="fragment" content="!">
```

For the second step, we need to use a server-side application to give a different answer based on query string parameters.

The specifications tell you how to give a full snapshot of the page when you get a request with _escaped_fragment_ inside the query string.

You can find many solutions out there, but depending on the website complexity you can choose between two different paths:

- Pre-render the pages and save them to the file system, and serve them instead of the normal page
- Pre-render the page on the fly (maybe caching them) when you get the request from the search engine bot

The first solution is easier if you have a fewer number of pages, or the pages are not updated often; you avoid managing all the infrastructure you should need to pre-render on the fly.

For our project, for example, we need to get only the main page indexed; it should be overwhelming to put on a server application with a headless browser (such as a NodeJS application using PhantomJS) to manage it.

The second option is the best when you have a very big website, with many indexed pages.

Anyway, in both cases, we need a web server serving different response pages based on the query string.

Here we are going to see how to do both paths with NodeJS, but the logic behind the process is the same independent of the web server you use.

Using a NodeJS server to return SEO pages

For this task, we need a web server to serve the pages; here we are going to use NodeJS; download it from http://nodejs.org/ and install it globally.

Instead of reinventing the wheel, we will use a package built for this reason: Crawlme.

Go to the CAPrapido folder, and then create the server server.js that we will use with NodeJS:

```
var express = require('express'),
    http = require('http'),
    crawlme = require('crawlme');

var app = express()
```

```
.use(crawlme({waitFor: 1000}))
.use(express.static(__dirname));

http.createServer(app).listen(8080);
```

With these really simple rows we ask NodeJS to load the three modules `express`, `http`, and `crawlme` for use and create a server listening on the port 8080.

`Use` means that for each request the logic from `crawlme` will inspect the URL for the text `?_escaped_fragment_=`:

- If it finds that, it loads the page with `zombie.js` (a headless browser), then puts the page into a cache, and gives an answer to the browser
- Otherwise, it simply lets `express` continue with the next middleware (`express.static`), which will return any resources found inside the folder named parameter to the browser

We are almost ready to test the web application.

In the `CAPrapido` folder, execute the following commands inside the shell:

npm install crawlme express --save

node server.js

Now you installed the dependencies to `crawlme` and `express` and started your server by executing the script using node, so you can try it.

You can see the differences between the following two URLS:

- `http://localhost:8080/`
- `http://localhost:8080/?_escaped_fragment_=`

As you can see, there are no differences, as we wanted.

 If you double-check the behavior, you can find differences, such as the Gender widget; the reason is that the page for the crawler skipped all the JavaScript, so it doesn't work with the keyboard like the normal one.

If you get differences between the two requests, it may depend on the loading time of the page; as you can see at `https://github.com/OptimalBits/Crawlme`, the function `crawlme` accepts a configuration parameter named `waitFor`, indicating how many milliseconds to wait before considering the fully loaded page.

With this simple code, you are exposing your web application and rightly managing the crawling for the SEO.

Let's check how to do the same when you want to pre-render the page by yourself.

Caching the page by yourself

Create a new server file `server2.js` inside the `CAPrapido` folder with this code:

```
var express = require('express'),
    http = require('http');

var preload = function(req, res, next) {
    if ('GET' !== req.method) return next();
    if (req.url.indexOf('?_escaped_fragment_=') === -1)
      return next();

    req.url = '/SEO' + req.url;
    next();
};

var app = express()
    .use(preload)
    .use(express.static(__dirname));

http.createServer(app).listen(8080);
```

Here we are using a custom function to manage the requests: if we find `?_escaped_fragment_=` inside the URL, we ask resources under the folder `SEO`.

Now we can simply open the page with a browser by ourselves and save the source of the page as `SEO/index.html`. Then, we start the server as we have done before, with:

node server2.js

Simple, isn't it?

You should check the documentation at this URL to better understand how what we have done works: `https://developers.google.com/webmasters/ajax-crawling/docs/getting-started`

Another good lecture you should look at is relative to a polyfill for `pushState`, because we are using it inside our application, and we lost the support for all the Internet Explorer 8; it is at: `https://github.com/Modernizr/Modernizr/wiki/HTML5-Cross-Browser-Polyfills#html5-history-api-pushstate-replacestate-popstate`

Summary

In this chapter, we built a Single Page Application with DurandalJS looking for accessibility and SEO.

We have seen how to use router and child router to better organize our modules, and a few binding handlers to improve the user experience.

We wrote standard markup that you have to write to create an accessible web application, and applied accessibility best practices to realize a widget.

Finally, we saw how to make the application crawlable by using NodeJS to implement the server-side logic (you could also have done this using any other server-side programming language).

Index

Thank you for buying
KnockoutJS Blueprints

About Packt Publishing

Packt, pronounced 'packed', published its first book, *Mastering phpMyAdmin for Effective MySQL Management*, in April 2004, and subsequently continued to specialize in publishing highly focused books on specific technologies and solutions.

Our books and publications share the experiences of your fellow IT professionals in adapting and customizing today's systems, applications, and frameworks. Our solution-based books give you the knowledge and power to customize the software and technologies you're using to get the job done. Packt books are more specific and less general than the IT books you have seen in the past. Our unique business model allows us to bring you more focused information, giving you more of what you need to know, and less of what you don't.

Packt is a modern yet unique publishing company that focuses on producing quality, cutting-edge books for communities of developers, administrators, and newbies alike. For more information, please visit our website at www.packtpub.com.

About Packt Open Source

In 2010, Packt launched two new brands, Packt Open Source and Packt Enterprise, in order to continue its focus on specialization. This book is part of the Packt Open Source brand, home to books published on software built around open source licenses, and offering information to anybody from advanced developers to budding web designers. The Open Source brand also runs Packt's Open Source Royalty Scheme, by which Packt gives a royalty to each open source project about whose software a book is sold.

Writing for Packt

We welcome all inquiries from people who are interested in authoring. Book proposals should be sent to author@packtpub.com. If your book idea is still at an early stage and you would like to discuss it first before writing a formal book proposal, then please contact us; one of our commissioning editors will get in touch with you.

We're not just looking for published authors; if you have strong technical skills but no writing experience, our experienced editors can help you develop a writing career, or simply get some additional reward for your expertise.

KnockoutJS Starter

ISBN: 978-1-78216-114-1   Paperback: 50 pages

Learn how to knock out your next app in no time with KnockoutJS

1. Learn something new in an Instant! A short, fast, focused guide delivering immediate results.

2. Learn how to develop a deployable app as the author walks you through each step.

3. Understand how to customize and extend KnockoutJS to take your app to the next level.

4. Great examples showing how KnockoutJS can simplify your code and make it more robust.

Mastering KnockoutJS

ISBN: 978-1-78398-100-7   Paperback: 270 pages

Use and extend Knockout to deliver feature-rich, modern web applications

1. Customize Knockout to add functionality and integrate with third-party libraries.

2. Create full web applications using binding preprocessors, Node preprocessors, and the Knockout Punches library.

3. In a step-by-step manner, explore the Knockout ecosystem by looking at popular plugins as well as the Durandal Framework.

Please check **www.PacktPub.com** for information on our titles

Web App Testing Using Knockout.JS

ISBN: 978-1-78398-284-4   Paperback: 154 pages

Design, implement, and maintain a fully tested JavaScript web application using Knockout.JS

1. Test JavaScript web applications using one of the most known unit testing libraries—Jasmine.js.

2. Leverage the two way bindings and dependency tracking mechanism to test web applications using Knockout.js.

3. The book covers different JavaScript application testing strategies supported by real-world examples.

Building a Single Page Web Application with Knockout.js [Video]

ISBN: 978-1-78328-405-4   Duration: 1:51 hrs

Create a complete and structured single page application by doing more with less code using Knockout.js

1. Create a well-structured and organized application that you can build on and expand.

2. Learn how Knockout's data-binding can help you do more with less code.

3. Make use of best practices to ensure a maintainable code base.

Please check **www.PacktPub.com** for information on our titles

www.ingramcontent.com/pod-product-compliance
Lightning Source LLC
Chambersburg PA
CBHW060555060326
40690CB00017B/3719